ARGUMENT

OF

JOHN H. B. LATROBE,

DELIVERED MAY 1ST AND 2ND, 1855,

IN THE CASE OF

ROSS WINANS vs. THE NEW YORK AND HARLEM RAIL ROAD COMPANY,

IN THE DISTRICT COURT OF THE UNITED STATES FOR THE
SOUTHERN DISTRICT OF NEW YORK,

BEFORE A JURY;

THE HONORABLE SAMUEL R. BETTS,
DISTRICT JUDGE, PRESIDING.

BALTIMORE:
PRINTED BY JOHN D. TOY.
1855.

THE following argument was reported with much accuracy by Messrs. Roberts and Warburton, of New York. In revising their report for publication, the object has been to condense, as far as practicable, the substance of what was said, without depriving it of its character as a speech to a jury, involving almost constant references to drawings and models. If those who heard it delivered, find any omission, it will be of that, which, although suitable at the time, perhaps, it was unnecessary to preserve: and if, here and there, an addition may be noticed, it will be found to be of something, which the desire of the Judge to have no argument on the law, prevented being said, or something that is inserted for the purpose of a fuller explanation, than, owing to oversight, or the rapidity of speaking, was given at the time.

J. H. B. L.

ARGUMENT.

WITH THE PERMISSION OF THE COURT,
GENTLEMEN OF THE JURY.

It seems to have been assumed that the summing up for the Plaintiff is to be a brief one.

Two days are left to me out of the six, which the Court has allotted to the discussion of this cause.

My promise to be brief, when the testimony closed, was made before the Counsel for the defence had piled up the mass of matter that now lies heaped before you as the argument to which I am to reply.

It is difficult to say, on what ground my learned friend supposes, that just one-half the time consumed by him will suffice for me. But, at any rate, I shall endeavor, gentlemen, to justify his anticipations.

In the outset, however, there is one thing, that I desire to have distinctly understood. I am here as the representative of Ross Winans, and of no one else, directly or indirectly. The allegation, made to rouse your prejudices, that this Patent is the property of speculators, is absolutely untrue. In 1838, the Plaintiff, as you have heard, sued the New Castle and Frenchtown Rail Road Company, in the Maryland District. He was then a person of very humble means, struggling against adverse circumstances.

He wanted the pecuniary ability to prosecute an extensive litigation. Years were, therefore, spent by him in fruitless negotiations for amicable settlements. Finally he employed Mr. Charles D. Gould as his Attorney, Mr. Gould agreeing to bear the expenses of the suits, and to look to collections for recompense and remuneration. This was in 1846. At the end of eight years, Mr. Gould, whose means had been exhausted in the conflicts which his agency involved, cancelled his agreement with Mr. Winans: and the latter, with the improved fortunes, which, under God's Providence, have, in the meanwhile, crowned his industry, now wages the present contest single handed and alone. The only interest that Mr. Gould has in the matter is a stipulated sum, to be paid to him out of the collections, as a compensation for the unrequited toil of those years of the prime of his manhood which he has wasted in the Courts.

And now, gentlemen, to the business more immediately before us.

You can find, a dozen times a day, the amplest illustration of the subject matter of this controversy at the corners, around which railway tracks are laid, in the City of New York.

Stand, for instance, at the corner of Centre and Grand Streets, and take notice of the cars that pass you.

First, there comes along the four-wheeled car of the city roads, unsteady in its motion, laterally as well as vertically, and taxing the full powers of its pair of horses to drag it round the curves. This is the type of the car used on rail roads before the eight-wheeled car came into existence. It is still the car of England, and of the greater part of Europe.

Presently, on the same track, the cars of the Defendants, on their way from Boston, make their appearance. They are upon eight wheels. They move with great steadiness. The four horses attached to them exert themselves less at the curves than does the pair of horses of the four-wheeled car; and yet, it is apparent, that they are more than double the size, much more than double the weight, and carry thrice as many passengers. These cars are those of which the Plaintiff claims to be the inventor. They have wholly superseded, except for street purposes, the four-wheeled car of Europe. They may be called, emphatically, the car of America.

Between these two kinds of cars, the most casual observer may institute a correct comparison, and understand almost at a glance, why one is better than the other.

Of the difference in the number of their wheels, their length, weight and capacity, we have already spoken. But there are other distinguishing characteristics.

The wheels of the eight-wheeled car are grouped, in sets of four each, at or near the extremities of the body.

These grouped wheels form separate bearing carriages, having a freedom of motion round a central bearing, that may be likened to the king-bolt of a common road wagon.

Looking upon these carriages as substitutes for the axles and their pairs of wheels in the four-wheeled car, it will be seen, that, while the former, as already said, are at, or near the ends of the body, the latter are considerably within them.

A moment's reflection furnishes the reason for this difference. Were the axles nearer the ends of the four-wheeled car, the work of the horses to drag the cars round the curves would be even greater than it is; indeed, it is evident, that, could they be put nearer together, without increasing the tendency of the car to see-saw, it would be all the better for the horses on the curves; and it is equally apparent, that if the bearing carriages were to be much further from the ends of the long-bodied car, the steadiness which is the result of their present position, in passing rapidly around short curves, would be materially affected.

Again, the closeness of the wheels of each bearing carriage, as compared with the proximity of the wheels of the four-wheeled car, is very striking: and it is at once understood, that it is this closeness of the wheels, while the carriage itself swivels on its centre, that facilitates the passage of the curves, as already mentioned.

Embodying, now, these details, for the purpose of a general view of the distinguishing features of the eight-wheeled car, as compared with its four-wheeled predecessor, and you see,

First. That it is more than double the length;

Second. That it is more than double the weight;

Third. That it is much more than double the capacity;

Fourth. That its bearing carriages are much further apart than would be admissible for the axles of a four-wheeled car, on a road having short curves, or curves of small radius.

Fifth. That the wheels of each bearing carriage are much nearer together, than would be admissible in a four-wheeled car, whether upon a curved or a straight road.

Sixth. That the bearing carriages conform themselves to the curves and inequalities of the road, without being controlled by the draft which is attached, not to the bearing carriage, but to the body of the car.

That there are these most striking points of difference between the two cars cannot be denied. That they are all in favor of the eight-wheeled car, is evidently the opinion of the public on this side of the Atlantic. This car is claimed by the Plaintiff as his invention. Should he be able to sustain his claim, he is unquestionably a benefactor of his country. This is the question, gentlemen of the jury, which we have been considering before you for the last two months, and which your verdict is presently to decide.

On the part of the Defendants it is insisted, that, if invention was involved, considering the elements at hand, common to all men, in the production of the eight-wheeled car, the Plaintiff was but the thief of other men's thoughts;—or, admitting him to have been an original inventor, he was not the first inventor, having been antedated both in Europe and America by those, who with the same objects in view, produced the same results;—or, that, if such prior inventors did not accomplish precisely the same results, they had nevertheless done so much, that common sense, without the exercise of the inventive faculty, sufficed for all the rest. These alternatives, with some matters looking to the abandonment of the invention by the patentee, cover nearly all that has been said by my learned opponent, during his four days argument.

I propose, gentlemen, to arrange what I have to say under a few general heads.
I shall enquire,
First. Whether the Plaintiff was the original inventor of the eight-wheeled car, as a whole, described in his specification.

10 ARGUMENT.

Under this head, will fall what has been termed the Baltimore testimony, forming, as it does, a distinct branch of the case.

Second. Whether the Plaintiff was the first inventor of the car in question: for he must, to succeed, be, not only an original inventor, but he must be the first inventor.

Under this head will fall the English inventions and publications, and the Allen, Jervis, Bryan and Fairlamb cars, so called.

Third, Whether, if the first and original inventor, the patentee has sufficiently protected himself by his specification; a matter in which we will require the assistance of the Court, whose duty it will be to inform you of the proper construction of the instrument.

And Fourth, Whether the Defendants have infringed the rights of the Patentee, and if so, the extent of the damage he has sustained at their hands.

And, now,—*First*. Was the Plaintiff the original inventor of the car which he has described.

It is necessary here that we should go back to the date of the invention, and the then existing and immediately antecedent circumstances.

The rail road system for general transportation dates with the Liverpool and Manchester Railway.

Baltimore had grown to be the third city of the Union under the patronage of the "pack saddle" of revolutionary times, and the influence of its successor, the Turnpike road. She was nearer to the Western waters, geographically, than either New York or Philadelphia. But when these cities compensated their deficiences in this respect, by the greater facilities which the Erie, and the Pennsylvania Canals afforded for cheap transportation, Baltimore was threatened, on their completion, with a fall as rapid as had been her rise. This was in 1826. For her, a canal across the mountains was an impossibility. The rail road system saved her from despair; and acting upon the report of what was doing in England, she planned and commenced the first continuous rail road for general transportation ever devised in America.

Gentlemen, I never visit New York without feeling prouder of my country. I never enter this great city—the great heart of my country, without feeling that the pulsations of my own heart are stronger and healthier. Nor am I the only Southern man, believe me, who thus appreciates New York. But, gentlemen, I must do justice to my own City of the South, and say that the rail road system of the United States had its origin in Baltimore, and that the Baltimore and Ohio Rail Road was the pioneer work of the country. The reason for this I have already stated. The reports of the Engineers of the Baltimore and Ohio Road were for years the *vade mecums* of the profession. All rail road inventors came to Baltimore; all new projects and experiments were tried there. The mass of testimony, in this cause, coming from Baltimore, the constant reference, throughout, to what took place in Baltimore is thus explained. It would have been strange, indeed, if between 1827 and 1833 any important step in rail road economy had been taken elsewhere than in Baltimore. New York and Philadelphia were satisfied with their canals. Baltimore's only hope was in the success of her rail road.

The news of what was doing "down South" travelled through the country. It reached, among other places, the hearth of a Sussex County farmer. It found his son, my client, and my friend, the white-headed man now seated at my side, young, active, enthusiastic and ingenious. He was already the inventor of the plan of fulling by steam. The public were besides indebted to him for the self-sharpening plough. He was not a person to hear of the new system of rail roads developing itself in Baltimore, and pay no attention to it. The friends of the existing and successful canals hooted at it. The loss of power by friction upon rail roads was the great argument against them. The question was a question of fact, and my client addressed himself to its solution. In the course of his experiments he invented this most beautiful application of the friction wheel, (here the counsel held up the model.) It is unnecessary to explain it to you in detail. This has been done by the witnesses. For the then speed upon rail roads, worked as they were by horse power, it was perfect. It has been called a "gimcrack" by the learned gentleman from Massachusetts, a term which has neither euphony nor elegance to recommend it. But it took the whole country, as it were, by storm. Its patrons were—so far as that man would take a patron—his patrons too. The Colts of Patterson advised him to go to Baltimore, the Mecca of such a pilgrim. The people of Baltimore appreciated his invention, and the Rail Road Company at once adopted it. The Jersey farmer's son became a man looked up to. He obtained a patent for his wheel, and with the introductions due to his ability and worth he went to England. He was present at the trial of the engines on the Liverpool and Manchester road which resulted in the triumph of the locomotive, and settled forever the question between Rail Roads and Canals. The friction-wheel excited so much interest there, also, that Mr.

ARGUMENT. 13

Stephenson, celebrated then above all living engineers, fitted up a car to compete with it, and was beaten in the contest. But the locomotive introduced a speed that was fatal to the Winans' wheel; and that, which was perfect in reference to the state of things at the date of the invention, was thrown aside when new developments in the application of steam substituted thirty and forty miles an hour in place of six and seven.

What had taken place in England was well known to the Baltimore and Ohio Road direction on the return of Winans from Europe, in June, 1830. Their own engineers had been present with him at Liverpool. The people of Baltimore, then struggling single handed with New York and Philadelphia for the western trade, had lost none of their interest in rail roads during his absence. They had not forgotten him or his experiments at the Exchange. He at once received employment from the Rail Road Company, and was charged with the improvement and perfection of their machinery. Among those who saw the most of him was the Treasurer, Mr. George Brown, of the great mercantile house of Alexander Brown and Sons; and nothing can better illustrate the deep interest felt in Baltimore in every thing connected with the road, than the part, which the testimony shows this gentleman took in its prosecution. He labored as though he were a day laborer engaged upon it, and acted in the outset as the superintendent of its work shops.

Gentlemen, this narrative is believed to be most germane to the matter in hand. We are considering the circumstances of the times, at the date of the invention. We desire therefore, that you should understand the excitement

14   ARGUMENT.

in Baltimore about rail roads—the cause of it, and the Plaintiff's connection with it.

Mr. Brown, then, being in charge of the machinery of the Baltimore road, and Mr. Winans employed to improve and perfect it, we come to Mr. Brown's testimony. In a conversation that he had with him, the date of which all the probabilities indicate to have been soon after his return from England, he, Mr. Brown, suggested how much safer an eight-wheeled car would be than a four-wheeled one. Mr. Brown's plan was two long beams with four wheels on each side. Winans at once made a rough sketch of what he thought would do. Here is the first direct testimony as to the invention—the suggestion of the idea of eight wheels by Brown—the development of it in a feasable shape by Winans.

In the following March, 1831, the rough sketch was exhibited in the shape of a careful working drawing, made to scale. The Company's car builder then was a coachmaker—you have had him on the stand—a young man he is called by the witnesses—named Cromwell, the elderly gentleman, now, so pertinaciously cross-examined by the Counsel on the other side. Cromwell swears that he received this drawing from the Plaintiff, and that a car was built according to it, which, when finished, was called the Columbus. Cromwell's testimony is clear and positive. But he is not the only witness. He is supported by Elgar, Fairbanks, Reynolds, Davis, Ferry, Lowry, Dempsey, Glenn, Cooper, Knight, Thomas, Brown and Latrobe.

These witnesses either heard Winans say that he was the inventor, or saw him giving directions while the work on the Columbus was going forward. About the details of this testimony, I shall not trouble you. With the excep-

ARGUMENT. 15

tion of Mr. Thomas now too old to be brought upon the stand, Mr. Brown too infirm, Mr. Elgar too ill, and Mr. Knight whose engagements made it impossible for him to be here, all these witnesses have been before you. Their testimony is relied on to prove, that the Columbus was built upon the plan of the Plaintiff, and after a drawing which he furnished to the coach builder, at the instance or suggestion of the Treasurer, and acting Superintendent of machinery, of the Company.

Gentlemen of the jury, with rare exceptions, these witnesses have been denounced, in one way or other, as unworthy of belief. Their credibility rests with you. At any rate we have produced them. We have afforded to the gentleman from Massachusetts the opportunity of cross examining them; and we doubt not, for a single moment, your reliance on their testimony.

Where are the witnesses for the defence, as regards the Columbus? On paper,—where all men are six feet high. Why are they not here? Who can tell me? Conduce Gatch—why is he not here? Tell me he will not come! Why, his business is a mill-wright's, working by the day. Double his per diem, and you can carry him to Nova Scotia. Gentlemen, the *Plaintiff* would have brought them here, had it been permitted, that the jury might have seen them, and that my colleague might have cross-examined them. No, gentlemen of the jury, the Defendants were afraid to bring them here. It was better to examine them in a commissioner's office, where the mistakes of the forenoon might be rectified in the after dinner examination; far better this, for the Defendants, than to put the witnesses upon the stand and oblige them to go through examination and cross-examination at a single heat. Gentlemen, I distrust the whole of the testimony that has thus been gotten up.

The Counsel for the other side has dwelt upon the effect of his cross-examination upon the witnesses for the Plaintiff. What did it amount to? It was a great consumer of time, and its plan was something like this:

"You say, Mr. Witness, that you heard Ross Winans claim to be the inventor of the Columbus?"

"I did."

"Will you be kind enough to repeat the words he used?"

"I cannot. The period is too remote. I cannot recollect words used in 1831."

"Will you repeat then, the substance of what he said?"

"The substance was, that he had planned, or invented, the car."

"Pray then, Mr. Witness, what was his language on the occasion?"

And when the witness again declined to attempt to repeat the Plaintiff's words, the learned Counsel placed him in the category of those who were unworthy of belief,—and commented upon him accordingly.

I do not know whether, in the chances of life, my friend is a bachelor, or whether he is a married man whom Providence has blessed with children. But assuming that he has a family, I naturally suppose that the welfare of his children is a frequent subject of conversation between their mother and himself. I know it is so in my own household.

And yet, I think that if he were placed upon that stand, and questioned, thus,—

"Have you ever spoken with Mrs. Whiting about the education or prosperity of William, or Mary, or James,"— he would indignantly answer, "assuredly I have."

"Mr. Whiting, will you name the times when you spoke to her upon the subject?"

"Well—it is a subject of common conversation between us."

"Will you mention the circumstances?"

"Well, really, I cannot,—we are always talking about the children."

"What were the words used, at any time, by Mrs. Whiting?"

"Really, Mr. Latrobe, you are very inquisitive. I know the fact to be as I state it, and I can say no more."

And, gentlemen, you can no more doubt the fact of Winans' claim to be the inventor of the Columbus, because of anything connected with the cross-examination of the Baltimore witnesses, than you could, in the case put by way of illustration, doubt, that parents had consulted about their children, though neither of them might be able to particularize the time, place or circumstances, of a single conversation.

But the drawing itself, handed by Winans to Cromwell, and from which the latter swears the first eight-wheeled car was built, has been produced before you. The Defendants charge that this drawing has been fraudulently gotten up. Do you believe this, for an instant? Why the very proof relied upon disproves the allegation. Witnesses have been examined to shew discrepancies between the drawing and the car as built, and the inference was that it had been made after the Columbus was completed. If so—then, why did it not correspond with the actual car. Fraud would have produced a more perfect counterfeit.

(Mr. Whiting—The argument states that the drawing was made in the course of the operation of making the

So much the more accurate should it have been—for there was the greater opportunity to make it so. The very discrepancies relied on shew that it was made neither during nor after the building of the Columbus. It was made, as proved by Cromwell, before the car was commenced; and the alterations in detail were, probably, the result of suggestions, while the work was going on—wholly immaterial, as they were, in any relation to the principles involved in the construction.

But Gatch, the mythic personage here, tells you that the only drawing brought to him by Winans was the drawing of *a body* of a car of unusual length.

How idle, this, and how shallow too! What was the object of making the drawing at all? It resulted from the conversation with Brown. It was to represent a car whose distinguishing characteristic was to be the *eight wheels* that were to bear it. Why, if Winans had done nothing but direct Gatch to make two bearing carriages, of four wheels each, to be placed under a long body, at the distance of one-fourth of its length, about, from each end, he would have connected himself as thoroughly with the invention, as he could have done by the most finished drawing exhibiting no more. What set Gatch to work on the two carriages for one body? He does not pretend that he began on his own suggestion. If he worked from the directions of another, that alone was sufficient to deprive him of all claim as an inventor. He is in truth entitled to no more credit than the spectator in the pit of the circus, who, when the crowd were applauding the equestrian performers, rose up and shouted, "by the Lord, I made their saddles."

But Gatch's testimony is easily explained. With him, the invention is not of the car as a whole; but of the trucks, or bearing carriages that form a part of it: and because he was the workman who built these, just as Cromwell was the workman who built the body, he has deluded himself into the belief that is apparent throughout his testimony. Nor is he alone. A much wiser man,—a far abler man,—the distinguished counsel from Massachusetts, participates in the delusion. He has asked the Court to instruct you, gentlemen, that this patent is for a combination of wheels very close together—united by a single spring, on either side of a truck—bearing the body of the car exclusively upon its centre,—three elements to be found in the trucks alone. We, on the other hand, insist, that it is for an eight-wheeled car, *as a whole*, whose distinguishing characteristics have already been described.

Should the Court grant the instructions which the Defendants pray for, we have no case before you. You need not leave your box to find your verdict. The Plaintiff, then, will have no standing here. And whatever may be your convictions about his merit in this behalf, the Court will have settled the law against him, and until its opinion shall be reviewed, he will be remediless in the premises.

We put the whole issue therefore, gentlemen, upon the Court's instructing you that the patent is for *the car as a whole*, and thus falsifying the doctrine, which, beginning with Gatch, has ended with the gentleman from Massachusetts.

But who is Conduce Gatch? I know him well. Rupp, too, and Forest? I have known them all. I find in the volume of printed testimony so often referred to, that their characters have been hedged around with affidavits. This was wholly unnecessary. No purpose was entertained of impeaching them. That they are ignorant men, speaking under strong bias, and whose wishes blind their memories,

I believe, but nothing more. My learned friend seems to think it his duty to gainsay the character of nearly every one whose testimony is adverse to the defence. Such is not my appreciation of my vocation as a lawyer. We have great immunity, gentlemen of the jury, great power as professional men. But our immunities should make us merciful in the exercise of our power, as regards the feelings and the reputation of witnesses upon the stand; and never, no never, should we, without strong necessity, by covert insinuation or loose remark, trample upon that most sensitive of all God's creations, the human heart. No such necessity has existed here, if my learned friend will permit me to say so, upon either side.

Turning then, to the testimony of Gatch, Rupp and others, what does it amount to? Absolutely to nothing, if we are right in our construction of the patent; because, not one of these witnesses seem to have looked upon the invention in the proper light; and all of them have based their opinions of Gatch's merit as inventor, not upon any appreciation on his part, to which they can testify, of the car, as a whole, but upon the fact of his connection with the construction of the bearing carriages that form a part of it.

If then, gentlemen, you put faith in the testimony of the witnesses for the Plaintiff, whose names I have enumerated, you must believe,—that the value of a car, for general purposes, on eight wheels, having been suggested to Winans on his return from Europe, he made, first, a rough sketch of the idea, and afterwards a proper working drawing,—that this drawing is the one that has been produced before you,—that it was placed in the hands of Cromwell in March, 1831,—that the car, called the Columbus, was built, in all important particulars, in accordance with it,—that the Plaintiff superintended its construction, and that it was put upon the road in the summer of that year. The same testimony will satisfy you, that Gatch's only connection with it grew out of his being the mechanic in charge of the shops where it was completed, working, at times, in person, on the trucks—and that all that he says to the contrary is to be attributed, less to an intention to mislead, than to the want of a proper conception of the nature of the invention.

Let us now look at the probabilities of our case, so far as they relate to the question of invention.

In the first place, Baltimore, for the reasons already given, was the city of the Union, of all others, in which it was most likely that such an invention would be made.

In the next place, Winans was a man of unquestioned mechanical skill, who had already devoted himself to the improvement, in New Jersey, of Rail Road machinery.

Again, he was in England when the question of such machinery occupied intensely the public mind.

He participated in the experiments that were being made on the Liverpool and Manchester road.

He returned to Baltimore to find the cars in use were imitations of the bodies of the stage coaches of the day.

He was at once employed by the Rail Road Company, and made the assistant of the Chief Engineer, in all matters appertaining to machinery.

The improvement and perfection of the cars became forthwith his duty.

The importance of a car on eight wheels was suggested to him, and he at once made a rough sketch of what it was thought would do.

Presently, a car, novel in its design, following in the order of time the employment of Winans, made its appearance on the road.

During all this while, Gatch was a workman in the shops,—a mill-wright by profession,—without opportunities,—with no relations to the machinery of the Company, except as manufacturer or repairer of four wheel burden cars.

And, now, what are the probabilities as to the invention and its author—the foregoing being the facts? Are they not conclusive in favor of the plaintiff?

Gentlemen of the jury, there is no room for hesitation.

But, it is said, that, admitting all that is here urged, there was no originality in the invention: that it was to be found in what have been called the Timber car, the Wood car, and the Tressel car, constructions existing prior to the date of the Columbus.

Now, it must be borne in mind, that the Columbus is far from being the car described in the specification. The wheels of its trucks were too far apart, the trucks were too far from the ends of the body, and the draft, being by the trucks, controlled that free swivelling of the latter which was required by the considerations set forth in the specification. Still, the Columbus was the germ of the perfected invention. Hence our claim for the Plaintiff, as its author.

Let us go to the Timber car, first.

This, as you know, consisted, when in use, of two common dirt or stone cars on which bolsters were placed, swivelling like the bolster of a road wagon, and on these bolsters rested the ark log, or timber, that was too long for a single car. To prevent the cars from being drawn from under the load, they were connected by a board, with a hole or slot at each end, which dropped upon the draw pins. The power was attached in the usual way to the draw pin of the forward car. After the particular load was carried, the common cars returned to their ordinary uses, and the Timber car, so called, ceased to exist. Not only was the Timber car a temporary contrivance and not a permanent structure, but its proportions depended upon the length of the timber to be transported.

You see here (said Mr. L., taking up a stick about two inches square and four feet long) a piece of heavy wood, that I have had sawed, nearly through, from either side, in a number of places, so that it is quite limber. Imagine it to represent an oak log, forty feet in length. Let me place these models of trucks under it so that it may rest nearly level. You see, at once, how much further from the ends of the stick the trucks are, than they would be, were this a car body properly strengthened instead of a limber log. You see too, that the longer the log is, the farther from the ends would the trucks have to be, in order to preserve it nearly level throughout its length. Let me now place the trucks in the position proper for the trucks of an eight-wheeled car. You perceive, at once, that the centre of the stick falls to the ground. (Mr. L. placed the trucks as he spoke in the several positions referred to, with the results that he described.) You thus have the Timber car and its teachings before you.

But what could the Timber car teach the Plaintiff? The object ultimately obtained, steadiness of motion in passing curves at high velocities, depends upon placing the trucks of long cars at or near their extremities. The teaching of the Timber car was the reverse; for the longer the timber, the further was it necessary to place the trucks from the ends. Even where the timber was comparatively short, its elasticity required that the trucks should be within the ends, about one-fourth of its length. The variable proportions of this temporary contrivance afforded no aid to one seeking the fixed proportions of a permanent structure.

Again, the free motion of the trucks in the Timber car was controlled by the draft. The coupling-board made each truck dependent on the other;—for, even when there was a slot, the forward car slipped under the load, so as to tighten it. When several of these cars, if ever, were in a train, the second controlled the hind truck of the first.

While, therefore, the Timber car may have suggested a crude idea, it was incompetent to do more: and had it been studied in the details of its temporary uses, it would have retarded rather than promoted progress towards the great ultimate result which is described in the specification.

This brings us to the Wood car.

Admitting, which we are far from doing, that the Wood car is the same as that described in the specification, it is antedated by the Columbus. This is a question soon settled.

Bennett and Cadwallader, among the few witnesses who are conceded to be respectable by the defence, swear that they hauled all the wood that was hauled over the road, when it was first used for such a purpose, in the winter of 1830-31,—and that it was all hauled in four-wheeled cars. That there were then no eight-wheeled cars of any kind on the road. The Columbus having been planned prior to March, 31,—and put on the road about the 4th of July, is not affected, therefore, by the wood cars, if Bennett and Cadwallader are right.

The defence insists, that these witnesses are mistaken in their date; that they referred to the winter, in fact, of 1829-30. Could this be established, room would be left for certain inferences, which, the defence alleges, fix the date of the eight-wheeled wood cars in the winter of 1830-31. Now which is right?

In the first place, the witnesses themselves have no doubt about the date.

But they are amply corroborated. The report of James P. Stabler, the very report referred to by the defence, states that there was no rail road track laid down, that could have been used for the purpose, until after the month of March, 1830.

(Mr. Whiting.—Pardon me a single moment. I wish to state, that I do not intend to interrupt the counsel, in any statements, of any kind, in the course of his argument. But after the argument is finished, I will call the attention of the jury to what is most important.)

Mr. Latrobe.—Whether you will have a right to do so or not, the Court will decide when the time comes. I want, now, however, to go on with my argument.

The Court.—Let there be no interruption. The counsel has the floor.

Mr. Latrobe.—It is no annoyance to me, your honor,—

Mr. Whiting.—Two or three misstatements I will call attention to by and by.

Mr. Latrobe.—Then let me ask the gentleman to take a note of what I am about to say.

From Baltimore to Ellicott's Mills there was no track completed until May 22d, 1830. In other words, there was not a foot of track laid, on which wood could be carried, in the winter of 1829-30. It is impossible, therefore, that this could be the year to which Bennett and Cadwallader referred.

Again, the ground of the inference as to the mistake of these witnesses, is found in the testimony of Rutter, perhaps another, who says that he saw wood on eight-wheeled cars before the Three Tun tavern in the winter of 1830-31, which would antedate the Columbus.

But, by referring to the Rail Road reports, you will find, that the plan of bringing the road into Baltimore was not prepared until the 3d of February, 1831—so that,—the Three Tuns tavern, being some half mile from the outer station, and within the city—there was no rail road in front of it, on which an eight-wheeled car could have been seen during the period spoken of—the winter of 1831-32.

Bennett and Cadwallader, therefore, are strongly corroborated in their statements; and the Wood car may be set down as a structure subsequent to the Columbus. It may be said, in passing, that drawing by the trucks, it had all the deficiencies, in this respect, of the Timber car.

My colleague, Mr. Keller, requests me to state, gentlemen, what I had overlooked, that Mount Clare, spoken of in the reports, is not the Mount Clare depot, also mentioned there, but the residence, some half a mile to the westward of the depot, of the gentleman, from whom the depot property was obtained, and after whom the depot was named.

NOTE.—After the Plaintiff's counsel had concluded his argument, Mr. Whiting read from the reports, to shew that there had been, prior to March, 1830, portions of track laid west of Mount Clare: one being a piece of track for flanges on the outside, that was afterwards changed—and one or two other portions to facilitate construction and excavation. The scope of the Plaintiff's argument however was, that there was no track, on which wood could have been transported, prior to March, 1830, which was not denied.

ARGUMENT. 27

We now come to the Tressel car.

In the Baltimore Gazette, of December 17, 1830, there is a notice of the fact, that the carriage and horses of President Adams, then on his way to Washington, were taken as far as the Relay House, about eight miles from the city, "placed on a tressel attached to one of the rail road cars."

Again, the same paper says, "We understand that the Rail Road Company have prepared several of these tressels by which wagons or pleasure carriages may be transported along the road without being unloaded, &c. &c. &c."

In one of the pay rolls of Conduce Gatch for the same year, there is this entry.

"Two trussels for the transportation of horses and carriage."

Neither the article in the newspapers nor the entry on the pay rolls describe these tressels; neither of them refer to the number of wheels in terms. "A tressel attached *to one* of the rail road cars," the language of the Gazette, would seem to indicate that the Tressel car was a common four-wheeled car.

It has been necessary to resort to oral testimony to supply this deficiency. Gatch, the common vouchee, is resorted to; and from his description it would appear that these tressels formed a regular body, supported on two bearing carriages, consisting of slatted sides, with ends that lowered on hinges to admit the carriage and horses.

On the other hand, Glenn and Reynolds, who recollect the circumstance well, speak of the whole affair as one that was gotten up in a hurry, on the spur of the occasion. They say that a common four-wheeled platform car was prepared for the horses, by putting a framing round it, after the fashion, as they describe, of a "post and rail fence," access being had by an inclined plane at one end,—while the carriage was carried on another car, to which it was secured by wooden cletes confining the fellies of the wheels.

Now which of these witnesses is to be relied on?— Gatch describes the stock car that came into use several years afterwards—a heavy, strong and expensive construction—the present eight-wheel car, in fact, for carrying horses, instead of men and women,—a structure not required for the occasion, taking far more time to make than the haste involved allowed, and applied to no other purpose than transporting a single carriage and pair of horses, a distance of eight miles,—for there is no evidence of what became of it, or that it was ever used again;—whereas, the contrivance, described by Glenn, was one that could be readily prepared, would answer every purpose, would cost but little, and the temporary character of which sufficiently accounts for its disappearance, after it had furnished the newspapers with the materials for a puff. Puff, by the way, was, at that early date, the breath of the nostrils, almost, of this, the first rail road corporation in the country, dependent, as it was, upon public opinion for the punctuality of subscribers, whose faith in immediate profits was already becoming lukewarm.

The probabilities, therefore, are, that, of the two sets of witnesses, those who speak of the tressel car as the temporary adaptation of a four-wheeled platform car to an especial purpose, are the most to be relied on. It is difficult to believe, that the eight-wheeled car of modern times appeared and disappeared with such necromantic celerity on the 7th of December, 1830. Gatch has probably confounded the car that was used with the modern stock car. Tressels are the rough benches used by carpenters. Trusses are the framing of bridges or other structures, supporting great weights between distant points. Neither tressels nor trusses, in common parlance, designate carriage or car bodies, or parts of such;—so that, without help from the term itself, we are obliged, in the conflict of testimony, to fall back upon, and be governed by the probabilities; and these, as we have already said, forbid our believing that the car, as described by Gatch, ever had any existence, until after the eight-wheeled car, perfected by Winans, had demonstrated its value.

Ross Winans, then, was not indebted to either the Timber, the Wood, or the Tressel car; but, so far as they are concerned, is to be regarded as the original inventor of the car Columbus,—which, planned after the conversation with Brown, in 1830, appeared in the smoked drawing, as it is called, in March, 1831, and was at length completed and put into use on the 4th of July of that year.

Starting then with the Columbus as the first attempt, and having shown that whatever there was in it, of good or bad, was due to Winans, we proceed with the history of the invention.

But, while the Columbus was used occasionally on the road, the testimony must have satisfied you, gentlemen of the jury, that it was comparatively a failure. It certainly did not encourage the Rail Road Company to take further steps immediately, in the construction of eight-wheel cars. In the language of one of the witnesses, there were those who regarded it as one of the "humbugs" of the day. It was altered in many respects, and, when excursion trains were run, was made to serve a purpose. But, on the whole, the car was unquestionably a failure.

A year elapsed before another opportunity was afforded to the Plaintiff to prosecute his invention.

In 1832, the Herald, a four-wheeled English engine, one of the first imported, was placed on the Susquehanna Rail Road, leading northwardly from Baltimore, and then in charge of Major George W. Whistler, afterwards eminent as the engineer of the great Russian road from St. Petersburg to Moscow. The Susquehanna Road was full of sharp curves, of radii as short, in many places, as 400 feet. The four drivers of the Herald would not pass around them. The engine was useless. Presently, Major Whistler sent the witness, Mr. Alexander, to consult with Mr. Winans. The difficulty was explained; and the next day, the latter produced a sketch, showing how a four-wheeled swivelling truck could be substituted for the forward drivers of the Herald. A truck was built, put under the engine, and the curves of the road ceased to be a difficulty. This was in September, 1832. About the same time Mr. Jervis invented the same contrivance for the English engines John Bull and Experiment.

It has been suggested that Winans pirated Jervis' invention. But this is idle. Had it been known in Baltimore, Major Whistler would hardly have sent Alexander to Winans, when he had Jervis to resort to, who had already mastered the difficulty. But Winans and Jervis were doubtless, both of them, original inventors.

The Herald brought into strong relief two considerations of great importance in the advance towards the perfect car. The proximity of the wheels of the trucks, having regard to the curves of the road, and the uncontrolled motion of the truck, which was a necessity of its use in an engine. The Herald therefore marked a step forward.

Improvement, however, marched slowly in these days. It was another year before Winans found another opportunity. In 1833, the Baltimore company, then engaged in the construction of their branch to Washington, became interested in determining the best form of passenger car, and Winans, still in their service, addressed himself to the enquiry.

It was the improvement of the eight-wheeled car to which he directed his attention. Cromwell was sent to the Camden and Amboy road; and returning to Baltimore, he built, under Winans' direction, the Winchester, so far in imitation of the New Jersey cars, that it was composed of three bodies placed on a single platform, supported however on eight wheels instead of four. The experience of the Herald told upon the construction of the Winchester. The truck wheels were placed close together and the trucks were left free—the draft being by the body of the car, instead of by a perch projecting from the trucks, as was the case with the Columbus. But the principle involved in the position of the trucks themselves, in relation to the body of the car, was not yet understood. Their position under the Winchester appears to have been determined by considerations of symmetry alone. They were placed under the centres of the outer bodies—farther apart, indeed, than the trucks of the Columbus, which were about a fourth of the length of the body from its ends, but still too nigh each other.

The Winchester, then, marked another step in advance—and there is no discrepancy in the testimony in regard to the Winchester being a far better and more useful car than the Columbus.

Then comes the Dromedary.

The idea had been suggested, of hanging the car so near

to the ground, that passengers might step in and out, without the aid of steps, or platforms. This could only be done on an eight-wheeled car, and only, then, by placing the trucks at the extremities of the body, which would be suspended between them; and accordingly this was the plan adopted by the Plaintiff in the construction of the Dromedary.

The trucks were now as far apart as they could be placed; and the advantage in ease of motion on the straight parts of the road, as well as around curves at rapid speed, was at once perceived. Symmetry, thenceforward, had nothing to do with the position of the trucks. Scientific principles determined it,—developed, if you please, accidentally, but none the less true or available, on that account.

And thus the Dromedary was another step forward. But this car was a clumsy one. No use was made of the spaces over the trucks,—and so the Comet was built.

The Comet differed from the Dromedary in several particulars. It consisted of five bodies, three of which were suspended between the trucks, and there was a body placed above each truck. Instead of a heavy framing, a bent and iron-plated side-piece supported the bodies—and, instead of the common bearing carriage, the wheels were united by the spring that is described in the specification. The Dromedary had been drawn by the truck. The Comet was drawn by the body. The Comet was a step still in advance.

But the suspended body of the Comet struck the angle of the inclined planes then used on the Baltimore road. And, to obviate this, the platform that sustained the bodies was straightened—the four bodies were placed upon a line, and the eight-wheeled car was perfected; and the Rail Road Company, with the experience thus obtained, ordered the cars for the Washington Road upon the plan, in principle and mode of operation, of the Comet in its altered form.

Gentlemen of the jury, upon this scroll suspended before you, I have had drawn the several cars I have described, that you may, at a glance, follow the workings of genius in the slow processes of invention. The human mind, in matters of this kind, rarely flashes forth results. When genius will condescend to work slowly, it works the truest. What better illustration can there be of this, than the scroll before you, gentlemen, affords. See here, in the Columbus the crude idea. See here, in the Herald, the construction of the free truck with its close wheels. Here, in the Winchester, the draft by the body—Here, in the Dromedary, the remoteness of the bearing carriages. Here, in the Comet No. 1, the simplification of construction,—here, in Comet No. 2, the whole invention developed; and here in the Washington cars, the true principle, and the graceful and convenient form, united into that, which, in 1834, established itself as the car of America—the car of the Plaintiff in this cause.

Gentlemen of the jury, I can make no stronger argument than this scroll exhibits. It tells its plain and simple story in language which even little children may understand. Truth is simple: and there on that scroll, is truth, in all its quiet simplicity, spread out before you.

From the completion of the Columbus to the perfection of the plan in the Washington cars, with one exception, it is not pretended that any living man, in Baltimore or elsewhere, was doing aught to improve or mature the eight-wheeled car, save Ross Winans. The exception is to be found in the testimony of Jacob Rupp, who pretends that the draft by the body was a suggestion of his own, made in the

34 ARGUMENT.

presence of Gillingham and Winans, and adopted by the latter. Fortunately, gentlemen of the jury, this witness dates his alleged suggestion. He fixes the date, beyond doubt, in March 1835. But the trucks of the Herald ran free in the fall of 1832. Witness after witness proves that the Winchester was drawn by the body in 1833; so was the Comet, in both its forms, in 1834; and Claridge, who identifies the time, by the death of his wife, from cholera, and his own severe illness with the same disease, swears positively, that one of the Washington cars, which we all know were drawn by the body, was finished about the end of the year 1834.

Gentlemen, this point, thus conclusively settled by the dates referred to, was deemed an important one by the gentleman from Massachusetts. To enforce it, he told you that it was in proof, that the draft by the truck was common, at first, to all the cars named, except the Washington cars,—the running gear of which, he alleged, was not finished until after the suggestion of Rupp. Fortunately for us, however,—otherwise it would have been necessary to establish the negative by wading through the whole mass of the testimony—the Court asked for the name of the witness, and it was given.

Turn we now to what Davis, the party referred to, has said in this connection. I read from the Stenographic report.

Mr. Whiting.—"How did the Columbus draw?"
Davis.—"By the truck."
"How did the Winchester draw?"
"By the body."
"How did the Dromedary draw?"
"By the truck."

ARGUMENT. 35

"How did the Comet draw?"

"By the body."

The counsel in his cross-examination then read from testimony given by the witness on another occasion, in which he said that the Columbus was altered to draw by the body, and asked,

"Was that the same with all the four cars?"

The scope of this question was plain. It was to lead the witness to say, or admit, that all the cars were altered to draw by the body, when the inference would have been irresistible, that he intended to testify, that all drew by the truck, as they were first constructed. But the witness, an intelligent man, understanding the bearing of the question, instead of answering "yes," replies,

"All that had been drawn by the perch."

The counsel then goes on, stating the fact interrogatively, "Were altered to draw by the body?"

To which the witness answers "yes."

That is to say, all that originally drew by the perch, to wit—the Columbus and the Dromedary, were altered to draw by the body. And the next question and answer remove all doubt as to this being the true view of the testimony, for the counsel asks,

"How was the Winchester drawn according to your recollection?" and the witness replies, "by the body."

I call your honor's attention to this, particularly. (Mr. Latrobe here addressed the Court.) The enquiry is an important one, according to one view of the case, and your honor's question, just referred to, gave additional point to it. The testimony of Davis utterly fails to support the allegation of the counsel. He examined it, doubtless, with less than his usual care.

Gentlemen of the jury, there is nothing then in the testimony which conflicts with the statement, now most emphatically reiterated, that in his progress from this stage of the invention to that, (pointing to the scroll from the Columbus to the Washington car) the Plaintiff in this cause marched alone. Unaided, save by the company, which, at rare intervals afforded him the opportunities, which his own means would never have enabled him to command, he marched alone—sometimes faster, sometimes slower, step by step, from the crude idea unto the perfected thought.

And even after his march was at an end, and his work was done, and his patent was obtained on the 1st October, 1834, who profited by his skill? No one save his immediate employers, the Baltimore and Ohio Rail Road Company, still the experimentalists of the system. His march had carried him ahead of the times, and before he could reap the reward of his ingenuity, he had to wait until the times caught up with him.

This is the proper place, perhaps, gentlemen, at which to refer to what may be called the Carncross, or Imlay car, which has been set up as the exemplar that was imitated, when the world at last opened its eyes to the merits of this great invention.

On one or two occasions during this trial, evidently with no purpose of giving offence, the learned counsel on the other side has spoken of the adroitness of his opponents. Now, if there is a word in the English language that I dislike to have applied to me, it is this same word adroit, which to my mind conveys the idea of doing something better left undone, or doing something, proper in itself, circuitously or underhandedly. The introduction of the Carncross or Imlay car illustrates adroitness both in manner and matter.

One of the Plaintiff's witnesses, Myers, having been sent from New England to Philadelphia to measure a car there, called the "Pennsylvania," occasion was taken by the Defendant, just as the evidence on both sides was being closed, to offer testimony, that the Pennsylvania cars, not the car called the "Pennsylvania," were copied from a car called the "Victory," planned prior to the date of the Plaintiff's patent, though subsequently to the invention of the Columbus. In all fairness, this testimony should have been introduced in the Defendants' opening, and not left to their reply. It was vital in one view of the case. Its introduction, at so late an hour, found the Plaintiff's counsel, except by cross-examination, unprepared to meet it. Mark, however, the result. The leading feature in the Victory was its suspension between the trucks, precisely after the fashion of the Comet, an original and very peculiar form of construction. The drawing of the Comet recalled it to the witness, with the difference that it was straight along the top. It was built, too, after the date of the Comet. Foltz, the pretended author, came from Baltimore. It was built, too, by Richard Imlay, who had been a car builder in Baltimore, in 1831 and 1832, moving to Philadelphia in the latter year, and doubtless keeping his eye on every thing connected with his profession in the city he had left;—Richard Imlay, residing in New York at this time, known to the Defendants, yet not produced by them. Putting all these things together, the result of the introduction of the Carncross car was this, that while Myers enabled us to trace the improvement, as used in Massachusetts, southwardly to Philadelphia, only, the course of the Defendants enable us to carry it to Balti-

38 ARGUMENT.

more, where the Washington cars, the perfected invention, were then in successful operation; thus justifying the assertion,—which, as I am a living and breathing man, I do most conscientiously believe,—that to the Plaintiff here at my side, relying on my feeble efforts in behalf of truth and justice, is our country indebted for the eight-wheeled car.

Assuming, gentlemen, that I have vindicated my client's claim as an original inventor, I propose to say a few words in regard to his alledged abandonment of the invention, prior to the date of his patent. The facts, here, connect themselves with the Baltimore testimony that we have been considering.

Many inventions are made which are never patented. They are abandoned to the public; and being once abandoned cannot be resumed. A patent, even if obtained after such an abandonment, is void. The Defendants insist that the Plaintiff's is such a patent. This is one of the questions, in regard to which you will require the assistance of the Court. It involves both law and fact.

The argument on the other side is this. Admitting that Winans invented the Columbus, yet having been put upon the road on the 4th July, 1831, it was his duty, if he intended to patent it, to do so within a reasonable time thereafter; and his allowing it to be used by the company, in its general business, without claim or complaint on his part, and until the 1st October, 1834, was such an abandonment of it as made the patent then obtained invalid.

The argument, as you perceive, assumes, that the car patented and the Columbus are identical. If this is not so, the argument of course falls to the ground.

That the fact is not as assumed, however, has, I trust, been thoroughly demonstrated to you; otherwise I have in

ARGUMENT. 39

vain called your attention to the slow progress of invention, step by step, through the Herald, the Winchester, the Dromedary, and Comet No. 1 to Comet No. 2, and the Washington cars, or those described in the specification. The true relations of the trucks to the body of the car, and of the wheels to the trucks, and the free motion of the trucks consequent on the draft by the body, all of them essential to the perfect car, are not to be found in the Columbus, but were the results of successive experiments.

In the Baltimore case, presently to be referred to, in 1838, this point came up; and the Chief Justice there directed the jury in substance, that, before there could be an abandonment, it was necessary they should be satisfied, that the Columbus, as well as the Winchester, the Dromedary and the Comet, were identical, in principle and mode of operation, with the car described in the specification.

We might put this point, then, upon the fact of the identity between the Failure of 1831, and the Success of 1834.

But the question of intention always enters into the enquiry we are making. And if you are satisfied, that Winans, from 1831 to 1834, was in good faith prosecuting his experiments,—

That they were of such a kind, as made him dependent, in conducting them, upon the facilities that the Rail Road Company might be willing to afford him,—

That he neglected no opportunity that was afforded to him,—

That the use by the company of the Columbus, and other cars named, was such an use as was necessary to test the value of his invention and improvements, practically,—

That, as has been proved to you by the president of the

company, the understanding with him was, when he entered into their service, that their shops and tools were to be at his disposal in perfecting his inventions,—

That the cars made by him as opportunity offered were not repetitions merely, but were bona fide attempts to make a more perfect vehicle,—

That the result was a vehicle far better than the Columbus,—the first rude suggestion,—

And that, as soon as the car was perfected, the patent was applied for,—

If you are satisfied on these points,—and there is no conflict of testimony in regard to them,—you must be satisfied, that, so far as intention went, there can have been no abandonment: but that the case is one, where an inventor, laboring to improve his invention before patenting it, is, unfortunately, in that position, which makes him dependent for experiments upon others, and where the experiments, which alone can demonstrate his merit, involve, necessarily, a use in public, liable to be mistaken for a public use.

I ask your Honor's attention particularly (continued Mr. Latrobe, addressing the Court,) to Judge Taney's opinion in the case of Winans *vs.* The New Castle &c. Company, to be found, as an Exhibit, in the Defendants' volume of testimony; and also to Curtis on Patents pages 47 and 344, where the law is well analyzed as regards abandonment.

But the testimony of Mr. Peter Cooper upon this point of abandonment, as well as upon the whole question of invention, is most important.

"Noble Englishman!" exclaims the counsel on the other side, speaking of Chapman, in connection with his obsolete contrivance. With how much more propriety might he not have exclaimed, "Noble New Yorker," in reference to your fellow citizen, gentlemen of the jury.

What was Mr. Cooper's testimony? Briefly this. Largely interested in real estate in Baltimore, he looked with anxiety to the completion of the rail road to the West. Presently, there appeared a work of authority, which asserted that steam could not be used on roads with short curves. The Baltimore and Ohio Road was full of such curves. Planned for horse power, it would seem as though it were unfit for steam, which had now come to be recognized as essential to the success of the rail road system. The friends of internal improvement in Baltimore were paralized at the intelligence. Doubts were entertained whether the stock of the new undertaking would not be forfeited. At this time Mr. Cooper addressed himself to the Rail Road Company. He undertook to demonstrate that the English author was in error;—that the curves of the Baltimore road did not prohibit the locomotive. Alone, unaided, with no other guarantee of success than his profound conviction and his strenuous will, he built an engine, not large enough to be called a plaything now, placed it upon the road, attached a car to it, and demonstrated his conviction. The company and the public yielded to the demonstration. Gentlemen of the jury, among the early friends of rail roads in Baltimore, who remember the discouragements of the times referred to, no name is more honored than Peter Cooper's.

This testimony of Mr. Cooper, therefore, gentlemen, is entitled to your highest consideration. He is no stranger to you. You know well that you can rely on him. He tells you, that from 1831 to 1835, his visits to Baltimore were frequent. He was constantly about the rail road establishment. He there found Winans, always busy.

He tells you, that he (Winans) was "employed as a kind of general mechanic, to meet and overcome the various difficulties that were constantly arising in the application of cars to the road, which they found very great,"—and that "he seemed to be at the head, directing and controlling their experiments;"—that his (Cooper's) acquaintance with Winans became intimate in 1830, and continued;—and that from 1831, for some years, subsequently, his visits to Baltimore were frequent, "remaining there sometimes three months at a time."

We thus connect Winans with experiments, looking to the very difficulties that were overcome by the eight-wheeled car, during the interval between the building of the Columbus and the Washington cars,—for Mr. Cooper recollected, as he told you, the intermediate structures. And we thus connect him, too, by a witness wholly unbiassed, and with the amplest opportunities of knowledge.

We trust that we have now established two facts in connection with this question of abandonment.

First.—That there were striking and essential differences between the Columbus and the perfected car—which make the ruling of Judge Taney full in our favor.

Second.—That so far as intention went, there was no intention to abandon, at any time during the progress of the improvement, from March, 1831, to October 1st, 1834.

And we contend, that the agreement with the Rail Road Company made them in fact the Plaintiff's agents in the use they made of the invention; and we rely upon the omission of all mention of the eight-wheel car, in the conveyance made to them, although at the time it was in course of being perfected, as proof, that there was no disposition, on his part, to peril, by a sale, his rights as its inventor.

The abandonment, prior to the date of the patent, being, then, out of the question, we proceed with the history of our case.—

As already stated, no one used the invention at the date of the patent, or for years afterwards but the Baltimore and Ohio Rail Road Company.

It is in proof, that, in 1836, it was introduced, against much opposition, partially, upon the Baltimore and Philadelphia road.

It was not until 1838, that there was an use that would justify a suit. The suit then instituted against the New Castle and Frenchtown Rail Road Company, came to be tried in 1839. It was well and thoroughly contested. The Columbus was urged as a prior invention, to antedate the patent. This led to the proof, that, whatever the Columbus was, it was the invention of Winans. Cromwell was hunted up, and it was found he had preserved the drawing. The Plaintiff and his counsel were alike surprised and gratified at its production. Its authenticity, then, was never questioned.

This trial in 1838, which resulted in the payment to my client of the sum originally demanded by him, although, the jury disagreeing, there was no verdict, gave him his first experience of law. For what purpose the fees of my colleague, Mr. Reverdy Johnson, and myself were dragged into this argument by the gentleman from Massachusetts, it is difficult to perceive; but it suffices to say in regard to them, that although moderate enough, they were a burden upon my client, which we would have lightened had he permitted us to do so. He was then laboriously engaged in building up the business, now the largest and best conducted in America, which has enabled him by its results to conduct a litigation like the present. In 1839, litigation, which he has been taunted with not pursuing, was a terror and a dread: and in the hope of being able to avoid it, he resorted to those attempts at amicable settlements that have already been referred to.

Of the temper and feeling of the Patentee, at this time, no better evidence can be afforded than that which is furnished by his letter to the Susquehanna Rail Road Company, which has been read to you as a portion of the testimony offered on the part of the defence.

Ultimately, as you have been told, Mr. Gould was employed, and suit was brought, convenient to his residence in Albany. This was in 1847.

Pending the suit brought by Mr. Gould, the patent expired on the 1st of October, 1848. Prior to this, application had been made for its extension for seven years, under the act of July 4th, 1836; and, in this connection, I propose to notice the argument, that the delay in litigation, already referred to, amounted to an abandonment subsequent to the patent.

Whatever delay there was took place prior to 1848, when the patent was extended.

Now there must be two things shewn before a patent can be extended. First, the Patentee must satisfy the office that he has failed to receive adequate compensation for the invention. Second, that this failure has not been owing to any neglect or fault on his part. A subsequent law subjects the patent to re-examination, as in the case of an original application;—so that in truth, all the questions here discussed, gentlemen of the jury, came before the Commissioner of Patents, in September, 1848.

The ordeal, thus prescribed by law, was passed through safely by the Plaintiff, and his patent was extended. The Commissioner was satisfied that there had been no neglect by the Patentee in the prosecution of his claims; and it is insisted by us, that, to this extent, his decision is final and conclusive: and if so, it settles the question of abandonment subsequent to the invention. The question of invention, indeed, still remains open to you, as it did under the original patent,—but the question of subsequent abandonment is precluded. These are matters, gentlemen, upon which the Court will instruct you.

The patent having been extended, the suit brought by Mr. Gould went on to trial, and resulted in a verdict for the Plaintiff. The verdict was for a nominal amount, to settle the question of right. But the efforts made to defeat the claim were none the less vigorous on that account. With the exception of the Quincy and Allen cars, all the matters that have been introduced into this cause were before the jury at Canandaigua. Among the dead, they had Chapman and Tredgold; among the living, Gatch, Forest and Rupp. My learned opponent has chosen to speak most disrespectfully of the trial at Canandaigua. It is true he was not of counsel on that occasion; but in his place was the late Samuel Stevens of this State. I never met Mr. Stevens but once. It was in the Supreme Court of the United States. His argument there was sound, lawyerlike and very able.

Mr. Whiting.—Did he lose his case?

Mr. Latrobe.—If victory is to be the measure of professional ability, how few of us can be looked upon as competent for employment. Gentlemen of the jury, I hope and believe that a feather will be taken by your verdict out of my friend's wing, if his flight heretofore has always been so fortunate that failure is unknown to him. Yes, Mr. Stevens lost the case I allude to; but the learned gentleman will permit me to say, that, from all I have been able to gather, the eight-wheeled car case at Canandaigua, was tried as well, in every particular, as though that gentleman himself had been present on the occasion.

Mr. Whiting.—I have no doubt of that at all.

Mr. Latrobe.—I am glad of that admission, because, unquestionably, from the beginning to the end of this case, the trial at Canandaigua has been sneered at.

The trial at Canandaigua was before Judge Conkling. On a motion for a new trial before Judge Nelson, all Judge Conkling's rulings were sustained, except one on a minor point, and the verdict was pronounced to be a righteous one according to the testimony. Our misfortune was, that the engagements of the Court were such, that a year, nearly, elapsed, before the decision on the motion for a new trial could be given.

A suit in Chancery immediately followed against Eaton, Gilbert and others. Time was necessarily lost in maturing this for a hearing. At length it came on in the summer of 1853, at Cooperstown. New testimony, not in the Canandaigua case, having been introduced, the preliminary injunction was refused; but it was a long time again before our turn came for the decision of our application. These are the chances, gentlemen, of litigation. Where Courts, like those of New York, are crowded with business, delay is a necessity. We have no reason to complain.

In the argument at Cooperstown, the peculiar tactics of the gentlemen now in charge of the defence, and who then appeared before Judge Nelson, were developed. You know them well, gentlemen of the jury. They have been made manifest before you. They consist in piling witness on witness to the same point, and then arranging them alphabetically in connection with the matters to which they testify:—tactics, so far effective, gentlemen, that Judge Nelson, in his opinion refusing the injunction, having referred to the preponderance of testimony, and his Honor, Judge Betts having permitted the accumulation to go on here, the Plaintiff was obliged to summon, from all parts of the Country, the witnesses, who, day after day, have been seen seated before you, that, man for man, we might be able to compete with our opponents—a sorry way of getting at the truth, gentlemen, but one, to which, at one time, we fancied ourselves obliged to resort.

The opinion of Judge Nelson having been pronounced in Eaton's case, now efforts had to be made. There was a suit in Equity in Massachusetts; there were suits on the docket of this Court, on the law side. It was determined to prosecute the latter; and notice was accordingly given. This has been called a hardship. We were asked to admit the mass of written testimony that had been prepared in the Boston case. We refused, peremptorily refused. For this we have been harshly blamed. We confess to no cause of blame. We resisted, in every way that legal ingenuity could suggest, the introduction of these depositions. Instead of being disposed to believe they ought to be admitted, I honored the ability with which my colleagues endeavored to exclude them, and tried to force the defence to produce their witnesses upon the stand. We had produced ours. What hardship was there in requiring them to do the same? We wanted to see how science upon paper compared with science in open Court. We wanted no echoes here. I promise you, gentlemen, before I have done, to shew how the mass of testimony was gotten up, that we tried, unsuccessfully tried, to exclude, except from the witnesses in person. We have had but one of the experts of the defence before you, Mr. Waterman. So far from hurting us, Mr. Waterman supplied a link in our chain. Every man of the Defendants' experts would have testified for us, as Waterman testified. For cross-examination did with Waterman, what it would have done with all the others. It brought out the truth.

The excuse for the non-production of their witnesses is entirely inadequate. Mr. Samuel Cooper not willing to come here for pay? no pay can induce him? He can write a treatise, in exaggerated terms, that fills forty of the pages of this volume, but cannot testify orally upon the subject! Eddy, a patent solicitor in Boston, will not come for pay? Shryack, a boss in the shops at Mount Clare, Smith, in the Lowell depot, will not come,—cannot be brought here? Idle and vain pretence! The Baltimore and Ohio Company runs two hundred and eight engines, and three thousand cars. Its road is four hundred miles in length, and employs four thousand men. Its master of transportation has been a witness for the Plaintiff on the stand. It could permit the absence of its master of machinery—its master of the road, who waited here for days, that truth and justice might be vindicated in the person of my client; and yet, to tell me that the foreman of the shops of the Lowell Rail Road could not be spared for a single day to come here! It is idle, all! Why, gentlemen, had the Plaintiff relied upon depositions, there would have been some excuse for him; but that the rail roads here represented in this defence, should do so on the ground of the difficulty of obtaining the attendance of

ARGUMENT. 49

the witnesses, can be accounted for but in one way—by attributing it to their apprehension of the result of the cross-examination, conducted throughout by my colleague. Gentlemen of the jury, that the Defendants have been sufferers from the course pursued by the Plaintiff's counsel, here, you cannot for a single moment believe. Every thing that ingenuity could devise, or activity accomplish, has been brought to bear by them during the trial: and looking back upon their efforts, our learned opponent can safely say, that not a point has been omitted, not an opportunity has been lost. Their preparation commenced long before this jury was empannelled. I hold here a volume of many pages. It contains the arguments of Mr. Hubbell of Philadelphia, and Mr. Whiting of Boston, in the case at Cooperstown—scattered in the interval broadcast over the land—one-sided statements, whose only effect could have been to give a bias to the public mind against the Plaintiff, and indirectly operate upon the minds of juries to his prejudice. And yet we are blamed for having forced them to trial under such circumstances!

(Mr. Latrobe here referred to the course of the Plaintiff's counsel, in cutting short the examination of their experts, at the suggestion of the Court;—commented upon the fact that the number produced by the defence had nevertheless been relied upon by the counsel on that side,—and then proceeded to enumerate and characterise those, who, but for the expressed wishes of the bench, would have been placed on the stand to testify for the Plaintiff.)

I have thus, gentlemen, brought the history of the eight-wheeled car from the beginning, down to the present hour; and I trust that I have proved to your satisfaction, that, from the crude idea to the perfected invention, Ross Winans is entitled to the credit; that he stands this day before you as one who has deserved well of his country; and that in claiming, at your hands, the reward which is his due, he has borne himself, directly, and through his counsel, fairly, honorably, and liberally, as one who loves the truth and is entitled to the justice that he seeks, in a verdict against the Defendants.

But it is said, gentlemen, that while he may thus be an *original* inventor, he is not the *first* inventor of the car that he has patented, which was either planned and constructed by others, or described in the various publications that have been offered in evidence. And this brings me to the *second* division of my subject.

The publications relied on are those relating to
    The Chapman Car,
    The Tredgold Car,
    The drawings and descriptions in Woods' Treatise,
    And the Fairlamb patent.
The prior constructions are
    The Quincy Car,
    The Allen Locomotive,
    And the Jervis Locomotive;
Each of which, by itself, publication or machine, it is contended, constitutes a sufficient defence to the present action.

We propose to take up these separately; but before doing so, let us enquire what end it was that Winans' aimed at, so that we may better appreciate the aid which they, or either of them, could have afforded him in reaching it.

When the Plaintiff returned from England in 1830, it was with the experience obtained on the Liverpool and Manchester Road, which was, virtually, a straight one.

ARGUMENT. 51

On this road, the speed which the recent introduction of Stephenson's locomotive rendered certain of attainment, was thirty miles an hour.

He was called upon to apply this experience to a road with curves of but a few hundred feet radius, that had been planned for horse power, and for a speed not exceeding six or seven miles an hour.

Peter Cooper had demonstrated, that short as were the curves of the Baltimore and Ohio Rail Road, they were not impracticable for the locomotive.

It was the duty of Winans, employed, as you have seen, for the especial purpose, to improve the machinery of the road, in view of the profitable use of steam upon it.

So far as passenger transportation was concerned, it was his business to devise cars that would pass round the short curves, as well as traverse the strait portions, with ease, safety and economy, at high velocities.

How this was to be done,—to what extent it could be done,—he was not informed. His duties grew out of the nature of his employment. The manner in which he might perform them was to depend upon his genius, skill and perseverance. No one could be his instructor; for the knowledge that was required did not, as yet, exist.

Had Winans accomplished nothing more than the building of four-wheeled cars upon the English pattern, he would have performed his whole duty. When he produced the eight-wheeled car, he did no more than his duty.

But, having regard to the scope and aim of our argument, the problem, in fact, before him was, how to construct passenger and other cars, so as best to adapt them, when moving at high velocities, to the necessities of a road with curves of but a few hundred feet radius. This problem was a new one; because the exigency that suggested it had now occurred for the first time.

The four-wheeled car, whose type is to be found in the cars in your streets, and whose disadvantages, especially in curves at rapid speed, have been pointed out, was the car in use in Europe and America. It furnished him with a starting point. Setting out from this, the result accomplished by the Plaintiff, in the solution of the problem set before him, was the eight-wheeled car, whose proportions and qualities have already been detailed.

I have here, gentlemen of the jury, a model of a four-wheeled car, so made that I can change the position of the axles. See now, when I place them at the ends of the body, and put the car upon this piece of curved railway, how great is the friction caused by the pressure of the flanges of the wheels against the rails, though, observe how steady the car is on the track. I move the axles, so as to bring the wheels close together under the centre of the body, and the friction of the flanges disappears; but now, the overhanging weight at the ends is inconsistent with safety, except at the slowest motion. Understanding thoroughly the demonstration of this model, the builders of four-wheeled cars always made a compromise between the extremes I have exhibited, and placed the axles about midway between the two positions, sacrificing, in so doing, something of steadiness and something of freedom from friction.

What the Plaintiff aimed at was to give the public the advantage of the remoteness of the wheels, as regarded steadiness, and of the proximity of the wheels, as regarded friction.

To this end he substituted a four-wheeled truck for each

axle, being able to place the trucks at the ends, because he permitted them to swivel freely round the centre, whereby the wheels conformed themselves to the curves: and he placed the wheels of each truck close together, being enabled to do so, because the body, no longer on four wheels, did not depend on the remoteness of the *wheels* for steadiness, but upon the remoteness of the *trucks*.

The slow process, by which he arrived at this result, I have already detailed to you;—it has been necessary for me to reiterate, however, the *modus operandi* of the invention, when perfected, in view of the continuity of my argument.

Briefly, then, but by this time I trust, intelligibly,—the remoteness of the trucks, the proximity of the truck wheels, and the free motion of the trucks around their centres, were the ideas, which, combined, solved the problem.

These were the ideas, then, that he was in search of.

What aid was afforded him in his search by the publications and inventions I have enumerated? This is the question.

And first as to the aid he received from Chapman.

Here are Chapman's drawings: and this is an honest attempt to execute them in a model. (The counsel here referred to a drawing and model.) There is no drawing of an eight-wheeled car, in plan or elevation.

Chapman's whole contrivance consisted in a scheme for working an engine by means of a chain. Sometimes the chain was fastened at both ends of the road,—a turn or two being taken round a drum on the machine,—the rotation of which, by steam or other power, caused the carriage to advance; or else, an endless chain was carried forward on a separate carriage, connected, as you see in this model, with the locomotive, and dropped into catches, that resisting the traction of the drum, produced onward motion.

You thus perceive that it was an *engine*, which Chapman, who was a ropemaker by profession, had invented. The maximum speed proposed by him was from six to eight miles an hour.

The engine, as described both in the text and drawings, is a four-wheeled engine. But, as the roads of that day were very weak, the inventor found that his engine might be too heavy for them, which would be a fatal objection to his plan. To obviate this, he suggested six wheels,—four of which were to be placed in a transome, as he called it, or bearing carriage, which turned on a central pivot, the motion being facilitated by friction rollers on the sides of the carriage: and if the six wheels did not sufficiently distribute the weight, then eight might be used, in which event, there would be two transomes, or bearing carriages. Thus, one thing is very clear. It was no part of Chapman's plan to invent a car for general transportation,—his only purpose being to *obviate an objection*, which he found might result *from the weight of his engine*.

Had Chapman's engine, therefore, ever been built, and had it been found that four wheels sufficed for it, six or eight wheels never would have been applied to it.

Chapman's sole object was to distribute weight. The idea of passing curves at high velocities, and the exigencies connected therewith, never entered his mind;—for high velocity was unknown. The only rail road transportation of Chapman's day was done in coal. Passenger cars were neither wanted nor dreamed of.

A difficulty that here presents itself, and which runs throughout the present discussion, is the difficulty of puting ourselves into the position of Chapman's ignorant cotemporaries. High or low, all were ignorant, in this connection, who knew less than he did at that time. Every thing is now so simple to us, that we cannot go back to the day when it was otherwise. We cannot, at will, forget. The courtiers of Ferdinand and Isabella remembered always the mode of making the egg stand upright, after Columbus had cracked the shell. We see what Winans has done. We cannot divest ourselves of our knowledge: and yet we must do so, to judge without bias in the premises. At all events, we must try to do so.

That we may deal honestly in this matter, gentlemen of the jury, let us see the objects which Chapman and Winans respectively had in view. This will go far in helping us forward in our search for truth.

Let us, afterwards, observe what was the result of Chapman's teaching upon his cotemporaries, that we may infer from thence what was its effect on Winans,—especially if we find that the former were as intelligent, and as alive to the subject, as the latter.

Chapman invented an engine to draw the coal cars of *that* day on straight roads, limiting his speed to six or eight miles an hour. Winans invented a passenger car, to be drawn over roads with four hundred feet curves, by the engines of *his* day, whose speed was thirty miles an hour.

Chapman, with a weak road, multiplied his wheels, not from choice, but from necessity.—Winans, careless of the road, multiplied his wheels, not from necessity, but from choice.

The result of Chapman's multiplication was the distribution of weight throughout a given piece of road. The result of Winans' multiplication was the concentration of weight at the ends of the same piece.

The distribution of weight saved Chapman's engine, which, without, might have been an impracticability;—The distribution of weight would have defeated Winans' car, by placing the wheels of the bearing carriages too far apart.

Concentration of weight would have destroyed Chapman's road; so he sought to multiply points of support, while the exigencies of his engine required *compactness* of construction.—Winans, influenced by exigencies that required *extension* of construction, sought to make two wheels operate, practically, as one.

The multiplication of wheels was what Chapman ended with.—The multiplication of wheels was what Winans began with.

As a consequence,—when Chapman made his suggestion, his work was done.—While Winans, beginning with the idea of eight wheels in swivelling trucks,—the extent of Chapman's contribution of thought to the subject,—labored three years before he produced the perfect car.

Would it not have been wonderful then, gentlemen of the jury,—if, with these antagonisms,—with different objects in view,—laboring to meet different exigencies,—Winans and Chapman had so far thought alike as to have produced the same result.

Men, with the same object in view, sometimes gain it by different means. But, men with different objects rarely hit upon the same means.

Necessity is the mother of invention.—The same necessities frequently produce the like inventions—different necessities never do: and the engine of Chapman and the car of Winans illustrate these truths.

ARGUMENT. 57

If there is a coincidence, then, it must be an accidental one.

But is there even an accidental coincidence, looking to the passenger car that was ultimately produced, in the elements that give to it its efficiency? These elements were the closeness of the truck wheels, as compared with four-wheeled cars—*in view of curves*, which gave *safety*—the lengthening of the body, and placing the trucks at the ends, *in view of high velocities*, which resulted in *comfort* and *economy*.

Was the idea of these elements, or either of them, to be found in Chapman? If not, then there was no coincidence, accidental or otherwise, in respect of our argument.

The drawings of Chapman are rude and imperfect. They are sketchy suggestions,—nothing more. In figure VIII, so much relied upon, the track is of different widths before and behind the car. The wheels are not at right angles with the axles, nor the axles at right angles with the body. The notion of applying scale and compasses to such drawings, with the expectation of accuracy in proportions, is idle.

Turn to the description for the elements, contiguity of truck wheels, and remoteness of trucks, of which Winans was in search. They are not to be inferred from any thing that is said there. An alternative construction, to meet a possible, and only a possible, contingency, is to be discovered in it, and nothing more.

We have thus dealt with text and drawings according to our present knowledge.

Let us now enquire, as we proposed to do, what Chapman taught the English, in 1812.

Our rail road system came from England. The English

were as alive to its value as we have ever been.—They spend by millions, where we spend by thousands, in prosecuting it. Chapman was in the midst of them. The Repository of Arts, containing his patent, was a work of universal reference. The English knew, then, all that Chapman had done or proposed to do.

The first evidence we have is afforded by Wood's Treatise, in the edition of 1825. Here, unquestionably, Chapman's suggestion is spoken of as a failure. How far the suggestion was availed of does not certainly appear, except from the drawing, which exhibits a compact engine supported on eight wheels, in two bearing carriages, the wheels being close together and equi-distant from each other, and the outer ones of the four, on the side of the engine that is represented, extending beyond the boiler, apparently from necessity. The power is applied to all the wheels by spur and pinion gearing.

This drawing, by the way, shows most conclusively, the incorrectness of my learned opponent's suggestion, that the length of Chapman's engine increased with the multiplication of his wheels,—for we here see the engine compacted, and the wheels brought as close together as possible to accommodate it, and yet extending beyond it.

I will not detain you, to read from Wood's Treatise, gentlemen: but counsel may refer to pages 144, 154 and 156, and correct me if I am in error, in my statement, that Wood proves that Chapman not only taught the English nothing, but that his suggestion of eight wheels was pronounced a failure by the authority the Defendants have themselves relied on.

But there was a second edition of Wood published in 1831, when the recent triumphs of the Liverpool and Manchester Rail Road had excited all England to the utmost: and would you believe it, gentlemen, that, in this edition, the drawing of the locomotive engine, *on two four-wheeled bearing carriages*, is omitted altogether! What a comment on Chapman's teachings, as the English appreciated them!!

And yet, gentlemen of the jury, these crude suggestions of Chapman's, which are thus shewn to have taught the English nothing, are relied upon as having taught the Americans every thing.

No, gentlemen! Winans wanted a guide into the regions of discovery. He found Chapman seated on the borders of the *terra incognita*, not dreaming even, of what lay within the mists that shrouded it; and he left him where he found him, and with no other guide than his own genius, no guard but his own courage and perseverance, he penetrated the obscurity alone.

So much then for Chapman and his teachings.

Before passing to the next in the category of foreign publications, I desire, gentlemen, to illustrate by the model before me, the meaning of the terms "concentration" and "distribution of weight," which I have so frequently made use of, in describing the difference between the purposes of Chapman and of Winans. It is most important that you should properly appreciate these terms. Much of the testimony has been addressed to their explanation. This model will leave you, at all events, in no doubt as to the meaning which the *Plaintiff* attaches to them.

Allow me however, first, to narrate to you an anecdote. It falls into the same category as the model, and will not be inapt as a preface to it.

A boy was, one day, standing on very thin ice, above

deep waters, watching his companions. A person on the shore saw that the ice was bending under the lad, and must yield, and in another instant, break under his weight, *concentrated* as it was, as he stood upright on his feet. So calling aloud to the boy, he told him to throw himself flat on his belly, or he would be drowned. The boy did as he was told, and the ice ceased to bend, as his weight, no longer concentrated on his feet, was *distributed* over the length and breadth of his body. "Now, you young rascal," continued the stranger, "squirm yourself ashore"—which was done, and the danger was at an end. The lad illustrated the principle of the Chapman car as he lay prostrate. Had he raised himself on his fingers and toes, arching his body, he would have illustrated the Winans car, with the weight at the ends—but he would have *concentrated* the weight at his extremities in doing so, and because of the weakness of the ice, the comparative of the road, might possibly have been drowned.

To return now to the model. This narrow trough, fifty inches in length by an inch in width, and some eight inches deep, is, you see, nearly half filled with water. Here beside it, is a row of blocks, less than an inch wide, each, by about six inches long, to the ends of which is fastened a piece of very flexible hoop iron. The blocks are as far apart as the sleepers, or cross ties of a rail road, on the scale of an inch to a foot. Raising the blocks, now, I place them vertically in the trough, the iron uppermost. Floating in the water, the blocks sustain the iron, as you see, upon a level. For the purposes of our illustration, the iron represents a rail road track, very sensitive and flexible—far more so than any rail road is, but not too much so for the truthfulness of the demonstration.

Having thus prepared the track, we must find a representative for a car fifty feet in length—on the same scale. (The counsel here exhibited a piece of wood an inch square, on one side of which were the equivalents of wheels, equidistant from each other,—the four wheels of one side of an eight-wheeled car—and on the other, the same equivalents, but placed, two at one end, and two at the other end, of the stick, in the position occupied in the eight-wheeled car.)

You see gentlemen, that when the wheels equi-distant from each other, are put upon the iron, it retains its level, *the weight being distributed equally along it.* Turning over the same stick, now, so that the wheels at the extremities may rest on the iron, you see that the level is, at once, lost, and the track arches upwards, until it touches the body of the car. This is the effect of the concentration of the weight, which is a characteristic of the Winans' car, as contradistinguished from the distribution of the weight, that Chapman suggested to obviate the probable contingency of his engine being too heavy for the rails. Which of these two modes of arranging the wheels does the most injury to the track, you may easily suppose, as the iron bars of the actual road transmit, over many sleepers, the weight that, for the instant, rests on any particular point upon the rail.

We come now to Tredgold, the next in the series of the English publications relied on by the defence.

(The Court, here, stopped the counsel, saying, that the usual hour for adjournment had arrived.)

When the Court met again, on the following day, Mr. Latrobe resumed his argument by referring to the water model, and further illustrating the principle, it was intended to exhibit, by reference to matters of familiar knowledge. He then went on.

And now, gentlemen of the jury, let us see what aid the Plaintiff could have obtained from Tredgold in his search for the elements of his eight-wheeled car—that is to say, the proximity of the truck wheels, and the remoteness of the swivelling trucks.

Here is the drawing of Tredgold, and here are two models alleged to be made in conformity with it. The one is the Plaintiff's, the other is the Defendants. Of the difference between them, we will speak presently.

The drawing represents, as you see, the side view of a long box car, supported on two four-wheeled trucks. The wheels rise above the bottom of the body; or, in other words, the body of the car, instead of being altogether above the wheels, as in the present eight-wheeled car, is sunk down between them,—so that, admitting the trucks could swivel, this lateral motion would be limited, as the wheels "brought up" against the sides of the body. The centres of the trucks are one-fourth of the length of the body from the ends, and the points of support of each wheel, on the rail, on the side exhibited, are equi-distant from each other. The relations of the trucks to the body, and of the wheels to the rail, are precisely such as secure the equal distribution of the weight over the length of rail corresponding with the length of the car.

There is no difference between us about these details. But we differ very materially about the fact of the swivelling of the trucks. The Plaintiff insists, they have no other motion than a vertical one, enabling them to pass from one plane to another. The Defendants insist, on the other hand, that they move laterally, as well as vertically, just as Chapman's transome did.

Now which is right? Many experts have been examined. But, gentlemen, this is a matter to be determined on inspection, and for this purpose all of you are experts. Look at the drawing. What other object has the small circle, under the four lines indicating the connection between the body and each truck, than to represent a bolt, or pin, passing through the side pieces of the framing, and permitting vertical motion only. How far do the wheels stand out from the body? The drawing does not explain. For aught that appears, there may be just room enough for the former to clear the latter, when of course there could be no swivelling, though there might be a free vertical motion in the trucks. Again, were the inner two of the four lines dotted, there might be some reason for supposing they represented a king-bolt. That the draftsman knew the conventional rule for representing an object, between which and the eye another object intervened, by dotted lines, is plain, for the part of the car behind the wheels is defined in that way. Looking then at the drawing, we find that the body is between the wheels, which is inconsistent with free swivelling—that the inner of the four lines are not dotted, as they ought to be, to represent a bolt—and that the small circle referred to can relate to nothing but vertical motion, and we come to the conclusion, from these facts apparent on the face of the drawing itself, that no swivelling was intended to be represented.

But turn now to the text.

Referring to fig. 26, plate IV., being that already described, the author speaks of the connection of the body with the wheel "frames, so as to allow the greatest possible change of *level* on the rails," which is just the sort of connection, which, we contend, is indicated by the small circles.

Mr. Latrobe proceeded here to illustrate the meaning of the words "change of level," by referring to the levels on the Morris canal, and the passing of canal boats from one to the other by inclined planes—the scope of his remarks being to show, that change of grade, rather than irregularities on the surface of the track, was meant by the author in the use of the terms "change of level," and afterwards, in the legend to fig. 26, where he referred to the axes of the wheels not being in the same plane.

Again, the legend to figure 26, is as follows. "A diagram to shew how a wagon may be made with eight wheels, so that the stress of each wheel on the rails of a rail road may be equal. The body of the wagon rests on the wheel frames at A, and is connected to them by an axis on which the frames turn, when from any inequality the axes of the wheels are not in the same plane. See page 94. See Diagram."

Does not this settle the question as to the meaning intended to be given to the word "axis" by the writer? The Plaintiff insists that it is a horizontal axle whose ends are represented by the small circles on the drawing, on which axle the wheel frames turn vertically. The Defendants, on the other hand, insist, that it means a pivot, around which the wheel frames may revolve or turn laterally. But "axis" is the singular of "axes"—"axes" is used a few words further on, thus, "the axes of the wheels"—"axles," therefore, or "axle-trees," in common parlance, are meant by "axes," and axis, the singular, must therefore mean an axle, or axle-tree, and not a pivot.

That this verbal criticism is just, is made evident by a

passage in the same volume, and in the same connection, where the use of six instead of eight wheels, is spoken of, and axis, in the singular, is used for axle-tree. This passage is omitted in the Defendants' extracts from Tredgold, doubtless accidentally.

That axis can mean pivot in one place, and axle, or axle-tree in another, cannot be imagined. "Axis," and "pivot," are common terms with different meanings, and Tredgold could not have confounded them. The learned counsel for the defence says indeed, that axis is a word well known to engineers, and means pivot. I frequently thought, during my learned friend's argument, that he assumed many things. He assumed a good deal of fact, a little law, and some philosophy. The meaning he assumes for pivot is to be found however, neither in fact, law, nor philosophy. "The axis of the earth"—who speaks of "the *pivot* of the earth?" An axis is a line, a pivot is a point. The jury can have no difficulty on this head.

I conclude, therefore, both from the drawing and from the text, that the bearing carriages of Tredgold's car had but one motion, and that a vertical one. And if I am right in this particular, the defence built on Tredgold, falls to the ground.

But, supposing for a moment, that I am wrong, and that the Tredgold car was carried on swivelling trucks—what can be more apparent both from drawing and from text, that the object of Tredgold was the distribution of weight. Nay, the author tells you so in express terms. Like Chapman, so far from looking forward to an eight-wheeled car, he seems to have regarded the eight wheels as an incumbrance, as is proved by his suggesting, as already referred to, their being reduced to six.

66 ARGUMENT.

What, then, was there in Tredgold to aid Winans in his search for the ideas that were to make his invention available. Now, that you know all about the subject, gentlemen, it is easy to take the drawing, and placing the wheels of the trucks close together, remove the latter to the ends of the body. But why did not Tredgold do this? What is there in his drawing, as we find it, to suggest that such alteration could be made?

Chapman's contrivance, for meeting the objection to the weight of his engine, is certainly not regarded by Tredgold as any thing extraordinary—though it is more than probable, that Tredgold, pillaging Chapman without acknowledgment, applied to general purposes, in figure 26, what the latter had intended to use with reference to a possible exigency of his engine only; with this difference, however, that Tredgold so little regarded the swivelling of his predecessor, that he abandoned it altogether.

Tredgold's silence in regard to Chapman is significant in our enquiry as to what Chapman taught the English about eight-wheeled cars; and the fact, that England has not yet adopted the car, is equally expressive as to the value, in the home market, of the diagram in figure 26, and its accompanying legend.

I cannot part from Tredgold, gentlemen of the jury, without reading a few remarks in regard to him, from the pen of Mr. George W. Smith, of Philadelphia, one of the leading witnesses proposed to be examined by the defence—a gentleman, whose testimony is not in the case, because, after he had been examined in chief, a domestic affliction prevented his returning to undergo a cross-examination.

Of the estimate placed upon Mr. Smith by the Defendants' counsel, gentlemen, you can have no question. It

ARGUMENT. 67

was certainly very high—second only, probably,—here I am in doubt—to the estimate placed upon Tredgold. Let me now shew you Mr. Smith's opinion of Tredgold. I read from Wood's Treatise on Rail Roads, American Edition, Edited by G. W. Smith, Esq., and from a note by the Editor.

"The work of Tredgold was made for sale and not for use, like Packwood's razor strops. As a practical work, it is worse than useless, abounding in erroneous statements of facts and foolish theories. The title is a misnomer. Mr. T. has invested his work with an appearance of profound science, and systematic arrangement. He has borrowed largely and without any acknowledgment from the work of Von Gerstner on Rail Roads, which was published in 1813, in Germany. The plan of the work and many of the details have been pirated. In the language of Mr. T. there are some *very singular* coincidences in this work also.''

And now, gentlemen, "when doctors differ"——though, I will press the point no further; but, placing this volume of Tredgold and the work of his commentator side by side, leave the matter of the Tredgold car.

The next in the sequence of English publications is Wood's work. This need detain us but a short time. It has been produced, I presume, because it represents a drawing of an eight-wheeled locomotive. Here it is, gentlemen of the jury, (the counsel held up the drawing,) and our learned opponent has said but little about it. The truth is, there is very little to be made out of it. I have already referred to it in connection with the Chapman engine, for the purpose of disproving the learned counsel's assertion, that length of engine followed multiplication of wheels in Chapman's mind. The drawing, if referrible to him, shews exactly the reverse, for the engine is as compact as it can be made, and the wheels extend beyond it at either end. But, gentlemen, the drawing is an important one for the Plaintiff, for it shews how little the swivelling feature of Chapman's engine-trucks was appreciated. Why, there are no less than eight spur and pinion wheels, "mashing" into each other, that the adhesion of all the wheels may be made available, in the traction of the machine; and to say that the friction, consequent upon this arrangement, is consistent with that free swivelling of the trucks, which attends the Winans' car, is simply an idle absurdity, and that is all. Let my learned opponent believe what he pleases about engines with cog gearing in New Jersey, they are not the engine in Wood's Treatise, nor at all like it; and if he will take the pains to understand their construction, he will see that I am right.

Like Tredgold, Wood's publication affords testimony to the inefficiency of the teachings of Chapman, and to the utter ignorance of the English, at the date of the respective works, of the true principles, as we appreciate them in America, of the eight-wheeled car.

Having thus gone through the English publications, I desire, before passing to the American constructions, relied on by the defence, to call your attention particularly to the testimony of one of the Defendants' witnesses,—which has a strong bearing upon both Chapman and Tredgold, and to whom, unquestionably, the Plaintiff is much indebted:— I mean Mr. Henry Waterman, the only witness of the other side that went through examination and cross-examination, as an expert upon the stand. To a remarkably fine and prepossessing *physique*, Mr. Waterman adds the *morale* of great intelligence in his calling as a mechanical engineer. His bias was certainly against the Plaintiff: his testimony, therefore, in the Plaintiff's favor is entitled to the highest consideration, when truth compels him to respond, as you will find he has done, to questions that go to the essence of this controversy.

I have been assuming, all along, that the Plaintiff's invention consisted in placing the truck wheels close together, and the trucks themselves far apart. I say, I have been assuming this. Now hear Mr. Waterman to corroborate me.

He is asked by my brother Keller—

"*Ques.* Do I understand you to say, that you define the invention described in the patent to be, placing the wheels in each bearing carriage close together, and coupling the two bearing carriages at remote distances from each other under the body, and bringing the load central upon the bolster, and the long side springs?

"*Ans.* That seems to be the substance of one of his combinations."

You will remember, gentlemen, that while the Plaintiff prefers the construction referred to in this question, he presents an alternative construction. Wherefore, the witness is asked,—

"*Ques.* What is the substance of the other combination?

"*Ans.* He says, the end he has in view may be accomplished by using the ordinary bearing carriage, provided the wheels are close together."

I beg to call the Court's attention to the foregoing questions and answers, as they may have an important bearing when your Honor charges the jury on the construction of the specification.

Now, it had been a part of the Defendants' opening to insist, that, no matter whether the wheels of a car were placed, as in this model of Chapman's car, that is, equidistant, or in groups at the ends of the body, as in the Winans' car,—the *distribution* of the weight was the same;—a point which we have denied throughout. Now, hear Mr. Waterman in regard to it.

"*Ques*. So far as regards the strength of the rails,—the distribution of the load upon the rails, which is the best adapted,—the distance between the wheels represented in Chapman's model, which is equal all the way through, or that represented upon the Plaintiff's car (Model C,) to enable the rails to sustain a heavy load?

"*Ans*. The Chapman model.

"*Ques*. Then was (did?) not Ross Winans' idea of the arrangement of the wheels in the truck, and of the truck with the body, tending (tend?) to concentrate the load at the ends of the car, instead of distributing it at four different points of division upon the length of the car?

"*Ans*. That was the result of his contrivance, whether it was his design or not."

You will doubtless recollect, gentlemen of the jury, a drawing, with reference to which Mr. Waterman was cross-examined. It contained three car bodies drawn to scale,—each fifty feet long. Under one, the wheels were placed as in Tredgold, in two trucks, one-fourth of the length of the car from the ends, and with wheels equi-distant from each other. This was marked A. B represented the same body, with no change in the centres of the trucks, but with

ARGUMENT. 71

the truck wheels brought close together. C, still the same body, but the trucks, with wheels close together, removed to the ends, as described in Winans' specification.

"*Ques.* Will not that drawing (A)* represent the distribution of the wheels under the body of the car, corresponding with the descriptions and drawings, both of the Chapman and the Tredgold car?

"*Ans.* It would represent one modification.

"*Ques.* Would it not represent what is described and delineated?

"*Ans.* It would not in the Chapman—*the wheels are too far apart.*

"*Ques.* But, so far as regards the distance between the wheels and their proportions relatively to the length of the car body?

"*Ans.* It would not change at all the distribution of the weight.

"*Ques.* Answer my question, and give your explanation afterwards. Does not that drawing represent the relative

* This diagram, which is essential to the appreciation of the examination, represents these three arrangements of the wheels with sufficient accuracy.

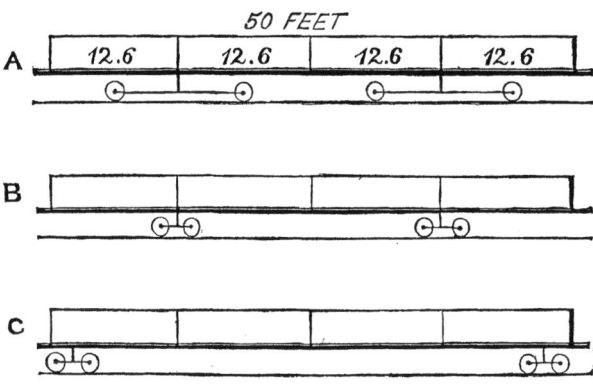

distance between the four wheels upon any one side of either Chapman or Tredgold car?

"*Ans.* I do not consider myself confined in Chapman's. He does not mention any thing in regard to it."

Now mark the force of this testimony. The witness has already said, that Winans' invention was in the relation of the wheels to the truck and the trucks to the body. The defence has insisted that the invention was obtained from Chapman; and yet we are now told, that Chapman is silent on the very point, where the defence asserts he was Winans' instructor!

"*Ques.* Answer my question, yes or no, and then give your explanation?

"*Ans.* It represents one modification of the Chapman car."

The witness did not see clearly where he was to be landed. He answered loosely here—he laid himself open to my brother Keller's next question.

"*Ques.* Where does Chapman describe *any modification* of the eight wheel car?

"*Ans.* He does not describe *anything with especial reference to the location of the trucks.*"

And yet, the location of the trucks is of the very essence of Winans' invention. Can there be teaching, gentlemen, without words or signs? There were neither here. What then could have been taught the Plaintiff?

But it was desirable that Mr. Waterman should admit that A was a representation of Tredgold and Chapman. Therefore, the question was repeated.

"*Ques.* Does this drawing represent the proper position of the wheels, to correspond with the Tredgold and Chapman car?

"*Ans.* I can only say that it gives one of the positions of the wheels in the Chapman and Tredgold car."

Diagram A, then, being identified, as it were, Diagram B is shewn to the witness, with close wheeled trucks far within the ends,—and he is asked, "how it differs from Winans;"—when he answers, "that the trucks are not near enough to the ends." He is then asked wherein it differs from Chapman, and he again repeats that "Chapman is not explicit on that point. *I do not know where he meant to place his wheels.*" He is then asked wherein it differs from Tredgold,—when his answer is,—"That the *wheels are too close together for the other proportions of the car*"—And yet, the learned counsel has occupied hours in endeavoring to satisfy you that the position of the wheels under the Tredgold car was, with the author of it, a matter of indifference!

The witness is then shown the Diagram C, where the wheels are close together, in trucks, under the ends of the body. The wheels do not touch, which, you remember, this witness said they should almost do, to meet the requisition of the specification. This will explain his answer to the question. "How does it differ from Winans?" "The wheels are too far apart in each truck." How does it differ from Tredgold? *The trucks are too far apart.* "How does it differ from Chapman?" "With regard to Chapman, I have said before, that he is not explicit upon that point."

Upon what point, gentlemen of the jury? Why, upon the very point which is of the essence of the Plaintiff's invention,—the closeness of the wheels, and the remoteness of the swivelling trucks.

And yet, Chapman and Tredgold are relied upon as all sufficient defences in the present action!

Have I not fulfilled my promise, that I would make Waterman the Plaintiff's witness?

What further did he prove that was important to us?

Why, gentlemen, who could have been more emphatic than Waterman, as to the necessity of placing the trucks at or near the ends of the car, looking to stability, and ease, and facility of motion in passing at high speed around curves; that feature of the invention so important to the Plaintiff?

(The counsel here read extracts from the testimony in corroboration of what he said, and explained why it was, that the farther the trucks were apart, the greater was the facility in getting the car round the curve.)

With a view, still further to simplify the subject, and make you understand how important is this proximity of the trucks to the ends in the eight-wheeled car—a matter to which, as we have seen, not the smallest reference is made either by Chapman or Tredgold—I have to ask your attention, gentlemen, for a single moment, to the model before you. I have a rail road track, as you observe, on a small scale, some six feet in length, which is inclined, so that the representative of a car shall slide down it. It is the effect of motion with differently arranged running gear that I desire to illustrate; and motion may as well be obtained through an inclined plane, as through the agency of steam, for my present purpose. A portion of the rail at the foot of the plane is turned obliquely to the general direction and is moveable, being kept in its position by a weight, which, after the moveable part has been disturbed, brings it back to its oblique position, the amount of the disturbance being measured by an index. Here are two wooden bars of equal length, size and weight. On one, there is a cross-piece at each end, placed in the position of the trucks of the common eight-wheeled car, with shoulders to keep it on the rail; on the other, there are similar cross-pieces, placed to correspond with the trucks of the Tredgold

ARGUMENT. 75

car, having regard to the length of the body. Letting the two slide now, successively, from the same point on the inclined rail, I beg you to watch the index, which responds to and indicates the extent of the motion of the oblique rail, as the cross piece strikes and slides along it. Do you not perceive, that it traverses a much greater space, when the rail is struck by the representative of Tredgold, than when the Winans' car slides down the plane;—owing to the greater difficulty of getting the one round the curve, than the other, measuring thereby the force of the impingement of the flange against the rail on entering a curve. (The counsel here repeated the experiment, several times, with the same result,—and then with a block representing a short car of the same weight; showing, in every instance, how much the ease and facility of motion around curves depended upon the length of the car, the proximity of the trucks to the ends of the car, and their remoteness from each other.)

My colleague, Mr. Keller, asks me to give you a reason for placing the trucks at the ends, which I had forgotten to do. When an eight-wheel car swings round a curve, the greater the distance of the trucks from the ends, the greater the space over which a given mass, the overhanging portion of the car, has to pass in the same time,—the greater the power, therefore, that is required;—or, practically, the greater the friction of the truck wheels upon the outer rail,—the greater the wear and tear of both wheel and rail,—the greater the liability of the car to leave the track when entering a curve,—and the greater the discomfort of the passengers in the car.

But, gentlemen of the jury, I might pursue illustrations until I wearied you, ending, at last, with what every child, who goes to the pump, can tell you, that the longer the handle, and the nearer to the end that it is seized, the easier "comes the water."

Finally,—with regard to these English publications. I have examined them by their texts and drawings; I have tested them by their influence upon the English, who, even yet, have no eight-wheeled cars; I have tried them by the testimony of the Defendants' leading expert; I have corroborated what Waterman has said by experiments before your eyes: and, gentlemen of the jury, may I not hope that your conclusion, like my own, is, that they, and each of them, were utterly incompetent to impart to Winans that knowledge, out of which grew the car described in the specification—knowledge, due neither to "Noble Englishmen" nor inquisitive Americans, if you please,—but to the talent, and painful, and laborious perseverance, against all discouragements, of the individual at my side.

And now we come to the American contrivances contained in the notice of special matter:—and, foremost of these, our opponents place the Quincy car, or, as it should be called, in honor of its author, the Bryan car: and it was an invention, gentlemen, to confer honor at the time.

Pursuing the same course of enquiry, we are now to find out the teachings of the Quincy car:—and first, were the ideas of the near and remote coupling,—using for brevity a phrase which, by this time, you will understand,—to be found in it?

Now, if the ideas referred to had existed prior to Winans' date, any where in America, it should have been at Quincy; because there were curves of but a hundred and fifty feet radius on the Quincy road, and cars of unusual length seem to have been required for quarry purposes.

The proximity of the truck wheels, as a means of facilitating the passage of curves, however, was not to be found in the Quincy car. There was no reason, in the size of the wheels, actually used, for not putting the axles near together; for the wheels were but eighteen inches in diameter, while the axles were five feet apart. This very beautiful model shews you the Quincy truck. For what reason, looking to its utility to the defence, I know not, its axles are so connected with a right and left screw, passing lengthwise of the truck, and worked by this portable crank, that the wheels can be brought into close contact with each other. But, although my brother Whiting screwed away at his model till he put the wheels into the position recommended by Winans—yet that was not Gridley Bryant's way of mastering curves; not at all. Instead of putting his wheels close together, *he left them loose upon their axles,*— so that the outside wheels, in passing a curve, being capable of travelling faster than the inside ones, it became unnecessary to resort to a close coupling, if Bryant understood anything about it, to obviate the difficulties of his crooked road.

Thus you see, gentlemen, that had Winans sought information at Quincy, in regard to passing curves, at speed, the loose wheels, and nothing but the loose wheels, would have been recommended to him. They were the only things he could have seen there.

Neither would Winans have found any thing at Quincy, to suggest to him the remoteness of the trucks, which the Dromedary first illustrated.

True, there were long columnar blocks of granite to be

carried. The cheapest and the quickest way to fit up a car for the purpose would have been to do, what my brother Whiting did, with such easy manipulation of his models,—whip off the short body, push the bearing carriages apart, and put on a long body. But it was left for my learned opponent thus to illustrate the capabilities of the Quincy car. When Gridley Bryant, its inventor, wanted to lengthen it, he went to the trouble and expense of making another eight-wheeled car, which he placed, end to end, with the first,—and then, putting his long body on both, one end of it on each, he produced what might be called a two storied car on sixteen wheels.

So that, the teaching of Quincy to Winans, as regarded a car of double the length, was, that it must have double the number of wheels; and had Winans taken counsel of Bryant, sixteen wheels would have been the recommendation of the latter, in all human probability.

Gentlemen of the jury, I would not willingly impute ignorance to Mr. Bryant. I would rather attribute what was to be found at Quincy to the necessities of his weak road, which permitted no other modes of construction; and the only fault I have to find with Mr. Bryant, supposing my brother Whiting ever did all this screwing and unscrewing in his presence,—is, that he did not say in substance, and at once, "my dear sir, this is all very easy—all very beautiful;—I only wonder, now, I never thought of it:—but the truth is, my mind was not in the track to accomplish anything but to work my quarry, carry my heavy blocks on my weak road, and make money for my employers." Had he said this, he would have probably told the exact truth, and saved us much unnecessary trouble.

Quincy, then, instead of teaching Winans to place his truck wheels close together, on account of curves, and his trucks near the ends of the body, for steadiness and capacity, would have misled him into the use of loose wheels, and sixteen of them into the bargain!

Gentlemen of the jury, before laying aside these beautiful models of the Defendants, it occurs to me to use them in an experiment on the Plaintiff's account, which could not be tried without them, and which connects itself with that part of the argument, that refers to the facility that the closeness of the wheels affords in passing curves. This is a fact, which is denied on the other side; or if admitted, it is done with a shrug, and we are told, that if it *is* so, yet, *practically*, it is of no consequence. Now I beg you to mark the use to which I am going to put the Defendants' model. The rail track is as well gotten up as the cars, and has just the curve in it that is wanted. I raise one end of the curved track, sufficiently to get speed on the car,—and, screwing the wheels close together, permit it to run down. You see, gentlemen, it performs its journey rapidly and safely. I now screw the wheels as far apart as the model will permit, and start the car. There it goes—eight inches, ten inches, a foot, a little more—and now it stops. I push it, it starts and stops again:—another push,—the same result. Well, but my learned opponent insists that there is a magic in the square of the track,—that is, in placing the axles as far apart as the width between the rails. Applying the screw, we obtain this relation of the wheels, and start the car again. Again it stops, when half way down; and, as you see, no pushing will aid it, unless it is continued to the end.

Why this model, gentlemen, after this shewing, was brought here by the Defendants, it is hard to say.

Pass we now to the influence of the Quincy car on the people of its day—the bystanders, as it were, around it. Let us deal with it, in this respect, as we have dealt with the English publications.

Who, after the people of Baltimore, were so eager about rail roads from 1832, and thereafter, as the people of New England.

The Quincy Road was, as Mr. Bryant tells us in his testimony, a pilgrim spot at that early time. What inspiration drew the votaries from the shrine?

Why, gentlemen of the jury, the Quincy car dates back to 1825. All New England was alive with the rail road spirit in 1832; and yet, there was not an eight-wheeled passenger car in all New England until 1838, after the invention had been perfected in Maryland, the patent taken out, and the Washington cars in successful operation.

And yet, Gridley Bryant was in New England. Curved roads required, in New England, what the curved roads of Maryland required. Four-wheeled cars were the best machines extant, ill suited as they were, to the public wants. Steam was flying in all directions. Gridley Bryant heard the thunder of the roll of cars and engines. But it loosened not the tongue that now prates so glibly on the subject. It opened not the reservoir of pent up wisdom at the time it was most wanted; and it is only now, after the long, long, interval of near twenty years, that Mr. Bryant tells us, that the eight-wheeled car of our country and the Quincy Granite car are one and the same!

No, gentlemen of the jury,—there is a limit to credulity. The judgment of Gridley Bryant's cotemporaries is against his pretensions; and, as he taught *them* nothing on the subject, we may fairly assume the incompetency of the Quincy car to instruct the Plaintiff in this cause.

ARGUMENT. 81

In this argument, I have dealt with the Quincy car in a way I have intended should be liberal. But, apart from all other considerations, the fact, admitted on all sides, that its trucks wanted the free swivelling, essential to the eight wheel car—being controlled by the draft—would be fatal to its pretensions as a valid defence to the present action.

In my opponent's manipulation of the Quincy model, he took occasion to state certain legal propositions, that require me to address your Honor, in view of your probable charge to the jury. (Mr. Latrobe here turned to the Court.)

It was stated emphatically, as the gentleman from Massachusetts shifted the bodies of the cars, substituting a long one for a short one, and *vice versa*, that a change in form or proportion did not authorize a patent; and assuming this to be all that had been done by the Plaintiff, he asked your Honor to charge accordingly.

But the learned gentleman mistakes the law. "Simply changing the form or the proportion of any machine" will not authorize a patent;—but, that a change *accompanied by new and useful results*,—when it ceases to be *simply* a change, will support a patent, I hold to be unquestionable law. I do not think my learned friend, as a sound lawyer, will venture, seriously, to deny it. I refer your Honor to the case of McClurg *vs.* Kingsland, in 1st Howard, 202. This was the case of a patent for casting iron rolls; and all that was done, in the way of invention was to give the gate, or sprue, through which the melted iron flowed into the mould, a tangential direction; whereby a rotary motion was given to the liquid mass; and the centrifugal force carrying the heaviest particles to the outside, the scoriæ were collected in the centre, where they did no harm, and the turning lathe always produced the smooth surface that was essential to the usefulness of the article.

Now, here was even less than a change of form or proportion. It was simply a change in the direction of a gutter: but it was accompanied with a new and useful result, and that made it patentable. So in our present controversy. If the change in the length of the car body, the relations or proportions of the trucks in regard to it, and of the wheels to the trucks, produced a new and useful result, and who can deny it, then our case comes precisely within the category of McClurg *vs.* Kingsland. I refer your Honor here to Curtis, pages 13, 14 and 16, for a good synopsis of the law in this connection.

Again, my learned opponent wants you to tell the jury, that, as this is a mere lengthening of a car body, therefore, it is not patentable. Now, in point of fact, it is a good deal more. But even if it were nothing more, still it would by no means follow, that my learned friend would be right in his law. If increasing length produces a new and useful result, surely it is patentable. The true test is overlooked—the new and useful result is disregarded on the other side. What is the lap of the valve of a locomotive, but a lengthening of the valve. And yet its effect is to cut off the steam, as it is entering the cylinder; and it becomes, in so doing, a most economical agency, as the expansive power of the steam is made effective. Illustrations might be multiplied; but enough, I am satisfied, may it please your Honor, has been said, to relieve the case from all difficulty growing out of the suggestions of the counsel on the other side, on this point of proportions. He has stated that this is a patent under the act of February 21st, 1793. So it is: and in that act the introduction of the word "simply," in speaking of a change in the form or the proportion of a machine, it is, of itself, sufficient to vindicate the law from the construction attempted to be placed upon it.

The next American invention in order of the defence is the Allen engine.

To this, gentlemen, I ask your particular attention. It presents a feature in the case that should be potential indeed, for the Plaintiff. We owe much to our opponents. Mr. Allen was upon the stand; and he there informed you, that the South Carolina Road, of which he was Chief Engineer, in 1831, and for some years afterwards, was a weak road, requiring the distribution of the weight of the engine on eight wheels; and that he therefore, planned, and had built at the West Point Foundry, such an engine, which may be described as two small four-wheeled engines placed back to back. (The counsel here showed a model of the Allen engine, and divided it into two.) An examination of the Defendants' model and drawings, gentlemen, will shew you, that in this engine, the cylinders were on the body of the carriage, and that the connecting rods worked crank axles of very large driving wheels that belonged to the trucks; and you have been told, what is apparent on inspection, that the free swivelling of the trucks was in this way controlled. This is not denied; but it has been insisted that this interference was immaterial; and that the trucks, notwithstanding, accommodated themselves to the curves. No doubt they did. But a control, to some extent, is admitted, and that is all that is essential to the argument.

We thus see, that the Allen engine falls at once into the category of those, whose only object was the distribution of the weight upon the rail with a view to the preservation of the latter. The ideas connected with the wants of the public in regard to passenger cars, that would travel with comfort, safety and economy, at rapid rates of speed, on roads having curves of but a few hundred feet radius, evidently, never entered into Mr. Allen's mind. As regards these wants, his inventive faculty was, unquestionably, idle. His car wanted the nearness of the truck wheels, the remoteness of the trucks, and the free motion of the latter. If he thought of the purpose accomplished by this combination, the combination itself was unseen by him.

Now what is it, in connection with this whole category of English publications and American machines, that we desire to prove? Why this? That an engine put on eight wheels to save the rails—a car looking to the mere distribution of weight in the best way, only,—do not, even with a contrivance for swivelling, more or less imperfect, make the transition from them to such a car as is described in the specification, such a mere dictate of common sense, as to involve no merit, and call for no exercise of inventive power, on the part of him who accomplishes the true result.—And to prove this, Mr. Allen is, perhaps, our most important witness.

In the first place, he is not only a man of common sense, but an engineer of the highest standing, whose deserts find their just reward in his eminent position.

In the next place, he was in charge of a road with curves of but four hundred feet radius, and his engine on eight wheels was in connection every day with four-wheeled passenger cars, so that a comparison between the two might be made at any time, whenever his eyes were opened to its importance.

Again Mr. Allen tells you, gentlemen, that frequently

when he desired to write, while the train was in motion, he went from the passenger cars to the engine, on account of the greater steadiness of the latter.

And yet, notwithstanding all this, when more passenger cars were wanted, he ordered four-wheeled ones!

Surely, this is demonstration. With all the elements before him, under the most favorable circumstances, Mr. Allen's failure to produce or suggest a steadier passenger car—a car that he could write in—can be explained but in one way, which is, that common sense was incompetent, of itself, to the new exigency; and that Mr. Allen, on this occasion, perhaps the only occasion of his life, was deficient in the inventive power, the genius, if you please, which was required by the necessities of the occasion, which distinguished the Plaintiff, and for the exercise of which he holds his patent and its extension.

To all, therefore, that has been said by the defence, in regard to the ability of mere common sense, operating upon existing knowledge, to produce the eight-wheel car, we oppose the undisputed facts of Mr. Allen's own personal experience.

He was "burning," to borrow a term from a children's game,—so close was he to the discovery; but unconscious of his proximity, with all his common sense he turned his back upon it, and, growing "colder and colder," commenced a search in an opposite direction. This we will now proceed to shew.

On the 16th May, 1831, while Cromwell was at work on the body, and Gatch on the running gear, of the Columbus, Mr. Allen wrote a letter, which has been relied upon as proving his perfect knowledge of the eight-wheeled car. But for the grave character of my learned opponents, and their thorough study of this cause, I should have looked upon the introduction of this letter as a jest, or a mistake. Recollect that the Defendants' argument is to shew that Allen *understood* and appreciated in May, 1831, the swivelling truck, as a means of facilitating the passage of curves of but a few hundred feet radius,—the truck, which is now used on the vast majority of American engines, and which is so important an element of the eight-wheeled car. As a matter of course, if he understood it for the engine, he understood it for the car: at least so runs the argument of our opponents. In other words, the argument is, that Allen had the knowledge, as well of the present uses, as of the future developments, of the truck in question, whether applied to car or engine.

But, gentlemen, I propose to shew you, from this very letter, that so far from appreciating the present structure,—so far from even understanding what Winans and Jervis did, subsequently, for the Herald, the Experiment and the John Bull, in accommodating these "locomotive carriages to the passage of curvatures," by providing them with swivelling trucks, Mr. Allen actually ignores what is now in universal use for car and engine, and actually recommends a system, which no one but poor Fairlamb has since dreamed of attempting, and which dispensed with the swivelling truck altogether.

Now hearken to Mr. Allen.—I read from his letter:

"No attempt has yet been made to accommodate the locomotive carriage to the passage of curvatures, by producing the means of *changing the parallelism of the axles*, and giving them *the relative inclination that the radius of curvature requires.*" There is no reference, here, certainly, to the truck, as the agent in all future success.

Mr. Allen then goes on,—"I consider it a point well worthy of examination, and not presenting serious difficulties. *I fully believe that on the Baltimore and Ohio Rail Road experience will compel them to have recourse to it.* Yes, gentlemen, this very road, on which this very Plaintiff was, at the date of that letter, toiling to bring to perfection, not the suggestion of Mr. Allen, out of which nothing ever grew but Fairlamb's patent—but the system which this letter of the 16th of May, 1831, is relied on to appropriate to Mr. Allen himself.

But listen, gentlemen, to what follows. "If it be asked," continues Mr. Allen, "why, with the views here expressed, I do not recommend the introduction of some such arrangement, I would reply, that no improvements, however much they may promise, can be effected without considerable expense and frequent disappointment." *Ecce signum,* (said Mr. Latrobe, suspending his reading, and pointing to the scroll of drawings from the Columbus to the Washington cars; then reading further) "all of which may, with a little patience be incurred and borne by others." *Ecce homo,* (said Mr. L. again suspending his reading, and pointing to the Plaintiff, near to him.) "The age, especially as regards this subject, makes its improvement *by the month,* and few cannot possibly pass by without contributing some important facts connected with it. And so fortunate do I consider the situation of the present undertaking, that I fully believe, *while it prudently gathers the experience of others,* it will, nevertheless, take the lead in transportation by the hundred miles with the speed and economy of rail roads."

Gentlemen of the jury, is it necessary for me to prolong the argument in regard to what Mr. Allen did, or to what his doings or his sayings could have taught? The failure of such a man—so very able a man—even when under the pressure of circumstances, to suggest any practical plan of overcoming an apparent difficulty, is the best vindication I can offer of the ability and merit of my client: and I have only to regret that while Mr. Allen was willing in 1831 to recommend the South Carolina Rail Road Company, prudently to gather the experience of others, he should have been brought forward in 1855 to prejudice the Plaintiff's claim.

I now pass to the Jervis engine, as next in order. Here gentlemen, I shall not say a word of my own. My sole argument shall be an extract from Judge Conkling's charge to the jury in the case at Canandaigua.

"One part of the evidence in the present case will serve to illustrate this. I allude to the deposition of Mr. Jervis, one of the Defendants' witnesses. The effect of it is to show that he devoted a great deal of time and thought before he succeeded in applying the four-wheel truck usefully to the locomotive engine. *Mr. Jervis is conceded to be a man of high endowments and of great eminence as a Civil Engineer.* I will read to you his account of the introduction and improvement of the engine on the Mohawk and Hudson Rail Road.

'I have paid,' he says, 'a great deal of attention since I have been connected with rail roads, to the construction of locomotives and cars. I have a good deal of knowledge of the principle upon which the running part of a locomotive and cars which are now used, and which have been in use since I have been engaged in my profession, have been constructed and used. My attention has been particularly directed to the subject of the arrangement of the wheels of

ARGUMENT. 89

locomotives and cars, to facilitate the running of locomotives and cars on curves; my attention was very early directed to that subject. It was a subject on which I had often thought a great deal, but made no experiments until 1831. In 1831 and early in 1832, *I was very much engaged in devising some means* by which four wheels could be substituted for two, as the leading wheels of the locomotive, and finally prepared a plan by which the forward end of the locomotive was supported by a sort of independent carriage, consisting of four wheels. These wheels were placed near to each other, and worked under the main frame of the engine, which rested mainly on the outside timbers on friction rollers, supported in its lateral position on the frame of the independent carriage by a centre-pin, and this independent carriage being a substitute for the two wheels formerly used.'

"Mr. Jervis, you will see, here represents himself to have been, as he doubtless was, an original inventor or contriver of the great improvement which he thus describes; but this was the year after Mr. Winans made a like application of *four-wheeled trucks to the Columbus*, and about the time of a similar *improvement made by him on the locomotive Herald*, as is testified to by Mr. Alexander.

"Now you have seen that both the carriages described in the English books, to which I have referred, are locomotives, designed, however, for purposes very different from the transportation of passengers over long rail roads; one of them is exhibited in the drawing with but six wheels, but the inventor has said that where the load was so heavy that it would injure the road, a double pair of driving wheels might be substituted for the single pair of driving wheels with fixed axles, and this suggestion is relied on by the counsel for the Defendants to disprove the novelty of the Plaintiff's invention.

"Now these books were equally accessible to Mr. Jervis and to Mr. Winans, and, considering their characters and the nature of the pursuits of these gentlemen, it seems not unreasonable to conclude that they were both acquainted with them. But we see nevertheless, from the evidence of Mr. Jervis, that it was only after long and laborious study, that he succeeded in making an improvement in the locomotive corresponding with that which it is insisted Mr. Winans made in the passenger car. The locomotive in use on the English railway, had one pair of running wheels on a fixed axle, as the passenger carriages both in England and those in this country (then few in number) had a single pair of wheels on a fixed axle at each end; and Mr. Jervis, after the earnest and persevering devotion of his faculties to the subject, and as far as we are apprised, with all the lights possessed by Mr. Winans, at length succeeded in devising and adopting a four-wheel truck for the support of the forward end of a locomotive, as Mr. Winans did in devising a like improvement for the support of each end of a passenger car. Now, with these circumstances before us, I must say, that it *seems to me to be requiring a great deal at your hands to ask you to say that there is no merit in what the Plaintiff claims as his invention.* But, gentlemen, it is for you to determine whether you find in it anything, substantially different from these other things previously in use."

And lastly, gentlemen of the jury, we have the Fairlamb patent urged by the defence.

The only result of Mr. Allen's suggestion seems to have been to set Mr. Jonas P. Fairlamb, of Philadelphia, to

ARGUMENT. 91

work; and we have a patent taken out by him, in which he describes a very original mode of making the axles of a rail road car conform to the radii of curvature.

Mr. Fairlamb's patent was one of those destroyed by fire in the Patent Office, in 1837. When he forwarded his patent, with a set of drawings to be re-recorded, the eight-wheeled car had for some time been recognized as a valuable invention.

The original patent makes no mention of more than four wheels. The specification is dated on the 29th December, 1832. When the new drawings were filed however, one of the figures on them was made to represent the application of the contrivance to a car on eight wheels.

In his affidavit, dated September 2nd, 1837, the Patentee does not swear that his drawings are copies of those originally filed, but that they are, "as he verily believes, a true delineation of the invention."

Taking into view, then, that his specification makes no mention of an eight-wheeled car, which was certainly of sufficient novelty to be noticed,—that the only part of his drawing at all matured, or referred to, in the specification, is of a four-wheeled car,—that his application of his notion to an eight-wheeled car, is rude and immature,—*that his invention was one, that would have made an eight-wheeled car unnecessary,*—and that Mr. Fairlamb's affidavit is so vague, as to warrant the idea that there was a purpose in making it so,—we are driven to the conclusion, that so much of his drawing as delineates an eight-wheeled car is an after thought, which occurred to him as he saw the car getting into vogue, and, naturally enough, felt disposed to show how his improvement could be attached to it.

And therefore, gentlemen of the jury, without further comment, I dismiss Mr. Fairlamb—and here close the examination of the English publications and American contrivances set up by the defence.

Let me now, for a moment, have your attention while I recapitulate.

Our patent was first offered. The defence was, that the Plaintiff was neither an original, nor was he the first inventor; or that, if either, he had abandoned the invention before, or after the date of the patent.

In rebuttal, we have, we think, established the fact of the originality of the invention, notwithstanding the testimony from Baltimore, by testimony at least much stronger from the same place, and by all the corroborating circumstances of the times. We have shewn, we believe, the priority of the invention by distinguishing it from all that had been previously done in England, or this country, in all the features, which characterize it, as described in the specification. We have made manifest, we trust, that there was no intention to abandon what was proceeding towards perfection in a series of successive experiments—referring to the use in public by the Rail Road Company, as a necessity of the occasion, looking to testing, practically, the value of the invention,—and we have explained the subsequent delay in litigation by giving to you the history of the proceedings, which have brought us, at last, before a jury of New York.

In my argument, gentlemen, I have endeavored, looking to the ground to be gone over, to avoid crowding it with details; seeking rather to fix your attention upon the leading features of the case, and to discuss the strong points on

ARGUMENT. 93

which it must ultimately turn, than such minor matters, as would, in my judgment, after all, be immaterial to the result. In this I have differed widely from my learned opponent. But every bar has its peculiarity; and that of Massachusetts, judging from the course pursued by its representative here, is a careful and laborious examination into detail, which, praiseworthy as it is, I do not feel competent even to attempt to imitate. Perhaps too, the picking up of the pebbles on the strand is not the best way of appreciating the glories of the spectacle as the sun sets upon the sea. But I may be wrong. Two days, however, as you can readily understand, were wholly insufficient to enable me to follow any other course of argument than that I have pursued.

The simplicity of the invention has been one of the difficulties that I have felt throughout. Now that we see it, every one of us fancies he could have invented it. Mr. Detmold, one of the cleverest of the Defendants' witnesses, looking at the Allen car, replied to a question, as to its being the same as the Winans invention, "the idea is there, if you start with the intention of finding it." Certainly, gentlemen; but then you must know what you want, before you can intend to look for it. So that, epigrammatic as was Mr. Detmold's answer, it amounted to nothing more than explaining his own position, which was that of a man, who, knowing all about the eight-wheeled car in common use, sees how he can convert Allen's engine into one, and cannot persuade himself that a stranger to the present system would have any difficulty in doing so. "The idea is there, if you will start with the intention of finding it," says Mr. Detmold. So was the woman's form in the block of Parian marble, before the Grecian Sculptor extricated by his genius, from her rigid prison, and gave unto the admiration of his own, and all succeeding ages, the Medicean Venus. So existed this western world, before the Genoese sailed from Palos with intent to find it. And yet my opponent would place the man who did but quarry out the stone, and the sailor who saw the sun go down into the sea without thought of the continent beyond, in the same rank with Praxiteles and Columbus. No, gentlemen of the jury, it is the idea, confined to one intelligence, the intent to find, exhibited in the action of the single individual, that constitutes invention; and it makes no difference, whether the result be "the bending statue that enchants mankind," a hemisphere with its continents and isles, or the car which now conveys its millions of persons, and tens of millions of treasure, along the iron highways of the land.

But, gentlemen, whatever may be your estimate of the merit of the Plaintiff in this action, however well deserving he may be of the rewards which the law bestows on the public benefactor, unless he can bring himself within the letter of that law, he is remediless in the premises; and I proceed therefore to my third division, and propose to enquire into the sufficiency of the specification, which lies at the foundation of the rights of the Patentee.

The whole theory of the patent law is to reward those who have deserved well of their country.

The universal practice of the courts has been to construe the law liberally.

The patent is not a contract, made by parties having mutual rights to settle and define.

It is a grant from the sovereign to the citizen, in the shape of a reward, and for the purpose of encouragement.

But to entitle the Patentee to the reward, which consist in the exclusive right to his invention for a specified time, there must be such a description of it filed in the Patent Office, as shall give to the public, at the expiration of the time, the information that shall enable them to use it. This is the office of the specification, accompanying the patent.

The Patentee must do three things to which the law prescribes.—He must let the public know what he claims.—He must teach the public how to construct it, if it is a machine;—and he must inform the public how it operates, to produce the proposed result.

It is contended by our opponents, that the specification is defective in all these particulars.

Whether this be so, is a question partly of law and partly of fact, and I therefore address myself in the first instance to the Court,—and I propose to enquire

First. What is it that the Plaintiff claims.

For the Plaintiff, it is contended that he claims—a car with a body of double the ordinary length, of those which run on four wheels, and capable of carrying double their load, supported on two four-wheeled swivelling trucks, placed at or near the extreme ends, the wheels of the trucks being comparatively very near together, that is to say, nearer than would be admissible in the wheels of a four-wheeled car for the same road.—The result being an eight-wheeled car, capable of pursuing a more smooth, even, direct, and safe course, at high velocities, over roads having curves of but a few hundred feet radius—than the four-wheeled cars constructed and in use ordinarily at the date of the patent.

For the Defendants, on the other hand, it is contended—

that the Plaintiff's patent is for a combination of three elements, to be found in the trucks only—that is to say—

First. Wheels close up to each other.

Second. Long springs connecting them.

Third. An exclusive centre bracing.

Or, to make the antagonism more apparent—The Plaintiff contends that the patent is for the car, as a whole—and the Defendants, that it is for a truck—a part of the car.

The Court sees, at once, that upon the construction of the specification turns the whole case.

It is sometimes necessary to go outside of an instrument, that the circumstances connected with it, and calling for it, may be used to aid in its construction. There is no such necessity in this case. The specification tells its own story throughout, and in the language of Judge Conkling "is remarkable for its perspicuity."

The specification may be divided into two parts: the first of which describes the new emergency, calling for the invention, to wit: the public demand for high speed on roads with curves of but a few hundred feet radius; and the second describes the means suggested to meet it.

And, then, after a reference to the four wheel cars in use at the time, and explaining the principles upon which the position of their axles under the body is determined, the Patentee goes on to say:

"The object of my invention is, among other things, to make such an adjustment or arrangement of the wheels and axles, as shall cause the body of the car or carriage to pursue a more smooth, even, direct, and safe course, than it does as cars are ordinarily constructed, both over the curved and straight parts of the road, by the before-mentioned desideratum of combining the advantages of the near and distant coupling of the axles and other means to be hereinafter described."

This is certainly very clear.

It is the body, that is to be made to pursue a more smooth, even, direct, and safe course.—The effect, whatever the means, is to be produced on the body. But, how? Why, by a peculiar arrangement of the wheels, that shall supply the desideratum of combining the advantages of the near and distant coupling of the axles and other means to be described.

In a previous part of the specification, the Patentee refers to *comfort*, *safety* and *economy*, as considerations, in this connection, of very great importance. Now, these are, all of them, considerations relating to the car, as a whole. *Comfort* is the comfort of the passengers carried: *safety* relates to this sort of transportation: and *economy* has regard to the number occupying, conveniently, a single car. But none of these considerations have anything to do with the particular form of the trucks under the ends of the body. These may be of the form preferred by the Patentee, or after the fashion of the common bearing carriages. Either form will gratify the description of the specification. Use which you will, with the eight-wheeled car, comfort, safety and economy will be the result.

It would seem apparent, then, from the scope and spirit of the specification, that the Patentee intended by it to cover the car he had invented, as a whole. The object of the law is to reward those who have done good service to the public;—that which confers the benefit, is what should receive the recompense. The car, then, and not the truck, is that which the patent should protect; unless, indeed, the language used by the inventor is such as to control absolutely the judgment of the Court. Were this not so,—were Courts to look at patents, to find how rigidly they might construe them,—they would be placing themselves in the category of those, who, instead of devoting their genius and toil to the promotion of the useful arts, employed them in contriving how they could best appropriate to their own use the labors of others, without either acknowledgment or compensation.

In asking your Honor, then, to construe the specification as covering the car as a whole,—we rely, first, upon the clear meaning of the terms used:—again, upon the spirit and scope of the instrument;—and, again, upon the fact, that it is the car, as a whole, that promotes the comfort, safety and economy aimed at; and that these are obtained, whether the truck is of the form preferred by the Patentee, or of the fashion which he suggests as an alternative construction.

A word, now, concerning the argument on the other side. This rests upon verbal and grammatical criticism. To understand it, we must read the claiming part of the specification.

"I do not claim, as my invention, the running of cars or carriages upon eight wheels,—this having been previously done; not, however, in the manner or for the purposes herein described, but merely with a view of distributing the weight carried more evenly upon a rail or other road, and for objects distinct in character from those which I have had in view, as hereinbefore set forth. Nor have the wheels, when thus increased in number, been so arranged and connected with each other, either by design or accident, as to accomplish this purpose. What I claim, therefore, as my invention, and for which I ask a patent, is *the before-*

described manner of arranging and connecting the eight wheels, which constitute the two bearing carriages, *with* a rail road car, so as to accomplish the end proposed by the means set forth, or by any others which are analogous and dependent upon the same principles."

The whole argument, it would seem, turns upon the proper antecedent to the words—"the before-described manner."

Emphasing "described," the Defendants' counsel would read it "described in detail;"—and there being but one description in detail in the specification,—which is the description of the spring truck,—he arrives at the conclusion that this is the proper antecedent: and that, in asking a patent for "the before-described manner," the Plaintiff asked for a patent for the spring truck, with its three elements,—very close wheels,—a long spring connecting them,—and a bearing exclusively on the centre of the bolster.

Now the value of this argument depends upon the necessity of a detailed description, to constitute a proper antecedent to the words in question.

But surely, it is too late to deny now, that *id certum est quod certum reddi potest*. Even Copeland, the eminent engineer, who testified for the Plaintiff, told my learned opponent, in reply to a question touching this very point,—"if you refer to a chain, you as thoroughly explain your meaning, as if you described it to be bars of iron, cut into lengths and welded into links connected together."

It so happens, that the specification contains two descriptions—one a general description of a car, the other a detailed description of a peculiar truck.

One of these descriptions, the Plaintiff, with certain objects in view, wanted to patent.

One of them would secure the object he had in view,—the other would not.

The general description of the car describes that which benefits the public.

The particular description of the truck describes that which the Plaintiff himself tells you, may be varied in fashion without affecting the result.

Then, which of these descriptions is it probable the Plaintiff had in his mind at the time he prepared the specification, and to which he desired that the words, "the before-described manner" should relate? May it please your Honor, can there be a doubt upon the point? Even could there otherwise be a doubt, is not the matter placed beyond all controversy,—resorting, now, to verbal criticism on our part,—by the word "with" in the same sentence. The Patentee might have stopped at the word "carriages"—when the sentence would have read—"what I claim as my invention, and for which I ask a patent, is the before-described manner of arranging and connecting the eight wheels, which constitute the two bearing carriages;" and had he stopped here, there would have been a firmer footing for the Defendant. But no! the arranging and connecting is not to be of the eight wheels among themselves, but the arranging and connecting these eight wheels *"with a rail road car,* so as to accomplish the end proposed."

If it were required to corroborate these views, ample corroboration is to be found in the prefatory part of the claiming clause of the specification.

The Patentee then refers to what had been done. He tells you it was merely with a view of distributing the weight;—that it was for objects distinct from those he had in view—objects, not even accidentally accomplished before his time. Whatever it was, then, that he did, had reference to new objects—to new results in rail road transportation; and if these results depended upon the car, as a whole, and not upon particular portions of it, as unquestionably they did, it must be to the car, as a whole, that his claim relates;—in other words, the antecedent to the words "the before-described manner" is the general description of the eight-wheeled car, and not the particular description of either the peculiar, or alternative, construction of the truck.

For still further corroboration of these views, I might refer to the testimony of the Defendants' principal witness, Mr. Waterman, who told the jury, in so many words, when examined as a mechanical engineer, in regard to the meaning of the specification, as it impressed itself on one skilled in its subject matter, that the essential invention was the nearness of the wheels in the trucks, and the remoteness of the trucks. He testified, as your Honor may recollect, that this seemed to be the Plaintiff's idea: and this, is the idea we ask you to protect, as the Plaintiff's property, in your charge to the jury.

Perhaps, it was to deter me from this line of argument, that my learned friend anticipated it; but at the same time, took occasion to say, that he would not impute to me the intention of using what was but a sorry subterfuge.

My learned friend might have spared himself the trouble of my vindication. The argument, he has called a subterfuge, is what I uphold as truth: and, what is far more in its behalf, is the argument, as I shall show, of Chief Justice Taney, of Judge Nelson, and of Judge Conkling, when the last named Judge was on the bench, and tried this case at Canandaigua. Subterfuge! May it please your Honor, my learned friend is not happy in his terms.

Assuming, then, that I have laid a sufficient foundation for doing so, I ask your Honor to charge the jury in the following words,—which, using the language of the Courts, with whose practice in the South I am familiar: I will call The Plaintiff's *First* Prayer.

"That according to the true construction of the Plaintiff's patent, he claims to be the first inventor of a car with eight wheels, arranged and connected, as a whole, in the manner, and acting upon the principles stated in his specification,—the object of which, is to make such an adjustment, or arrangement of the wheels and axles, as shall cause the body of the car to pursue a more smooth, even, direct and safe course, both over the curved and straight parts of a rail road."

By referring to the instructions to the jury in the Maryland case, your Honor will find that I have pursued the very language of the Chief Justice, with the single addition of the words "as a whole," which I have taken from the opinion which Judge Nelson pronounced, when he refused a new trial in the Canandaigua case.*

---

* At this place in the argument, the counsel was interrupted by the Court, and the following remarks were made,—ending with Mr. Latrobe's abandoning the discussion of the law, and addressing himself to the jury. But as an argument in a cause like this—wherein no notice is taken of the law, and no instructions are prayed to be given to the jury,—is, to one accustomed to practice in Maryland, very much like "Shakspeare's play of the Prince of Denmark with the part of Hamlet omitted"—the argument that would have been made is here and there suggested, as though in fact delivered—the justification being a desire that the whole report may appear consistent; and there being a precedent in the Halls of Legislation, if not in the Courts of Justice, for the publication of what might be called constructive argumentation.   J. H. B. L.

The Court.—If I hear these points discussed on your side, then I am bound to grant the other party an opportunity to discuss the propositions of law. But this business must be managed with some view to practicability. The argument

ARGUMENT. 103

Judge Taney's meaning is very plainly to be seen in his second instruction. Had he intended to confine the patent to the trucks, he would not have spoken of them as being

must close to-day; but if you argue half an hour or so upon the specification, pointing out the legal construction that you claim, and refer to your authorities, then the other side will expect to answer. In order that they should have the slightest benefit, the Court should take time to consider the points which would render it necessary to defer the charge after the close of the argument. You must either rely upon the written propositions you have submitted or submit others. Those you have submitted I have already gone over.

Mr. Latrobe.—I will then pass by, at the suggestion of the Court, that part of my argument, that I had intended to make upon the specification. Your Honor will do me the justice to say, that you have made no suggestion during the progress of the trial, with a view to shorten the speeches, to which I have not most cordially acceded.

The Court.—I was going to add, that, in the early stage of the case, I had personally a preference to the mode of presenting such complicated cases to the jury, pursued in some of the Southern Courts, over that which is practiced here. I think if the gentlemen had argued the propositions of law at the beginning, and given me an opportunity to decide upon them, the result might have been to abridge this trial. But now, to ask me impromptu, to meet all these multiplied and intricate questions of law, would certainly not be a pleasant matter.

Mr. Latrobe.—I will not pursue this part of the argument any further. Your Honor has already my nine or ten propositions, and I will only refer to the decision of Chief Justice Taney upon one point. He places the Columbus, the Winchester, the Dromedary and the Comet, in antagonism to the car described by the Patentee, which he would not have done if he had not looked upon the patent as for a whole car. He then places the Timber car in antagonism to the claim of the Patentee, which he would not have done had he not looked upon the claim of the Patentee, as for a whole car. Again, he speaks of the patent as a patent for a machine, and he uses the term machine—

The Court.—It should be obvious to the counsel that I could not discharge my duty by examining the opinion of Chief Justice Taney and Judges Nelson and Conkling, I could not give them that perusal which would be necessary with a view to legal results. Besides, so far as my impression goes, it is arrived at already in my mind; and I am prepared, at any instant, to make my remarks to the jury, after the close of the argument.

Mr. Latrobe.—Then I will go no further, but address myself again to the jury.

well known, nor would he have spoken of the invention that was patented as a machine, which is an aggregate of parts, not a part of an aggregate! And again, Judge Taney, in his fourth, fifth and sixth instructions, antagonizes the Columbus, Winchester, Dromedary and Comet,—cars, existing, as a whole, each, with the car patented, as a whole.

Judge Conkling said, "that the patent was valid if the Plaintiff's car was substantially on the whole, a new and useful thing."

Judge Nelson in the opinion already referred to, on the motion for a new trial says.

"His claim is for the car itself, constructed and arranged as described in the specification."

"The question is, whether or not cars or carriages for running on Rail Roads, as a whole, substantially like that described in the patent, had been before known,—not whether certain parts are, or are not, substantially similar."

Again, in view of the argument now made for the defence, Judge Nelson says:

"The argument presupposes that the claim is for the discovery of a new combination and arrangement of certain instruments and materials, by means of which a car is constructed of a given utility; and that if any one or more of the supposed combinations turn out to be old, the patent is invalid. This is the principle upon which much of the defence has been placed, but no such claim is found in the patent; no particular combination or arrangement is pointed out as new, or claimed as such. The novelty of the discovery is placed upon no such ground; on the contrary, the result of the entire arrangement and adjustment of the several parts described, namely, the rail road car complete, and fit for use, is the thing pointed out and claimed as new.

This is the view taken by the Chief Justice of the patent, in the case of the present Plaintiff, against the 'Newcastle and Frenchtown Turnpike and Rail Road Company,' tried before him in the Maryland Circuit, and which was adopted by the Judge in the trial of this case."

Afterwards, at Cooperstown—after hearing my opponent's argument,—the same that has been made here, Judge Nelson says:

"As we *heard* when the patent was formerly before us, the improvement claimed is the car itself, arranged and constructed as described in the patent, and which we have above, in substance, set forth; and the question now before us is the same as was before the jury in the former case, namely, whether or not cars or carriages for running on rail roads, as a whole, like the one described in the patent, had been before known or in public use? And whether or not, the cars manufactured by the Defendants are, in arrangement and construction substantially like it?"

Judge Taney's instruction, which the first prayer in this case follows, speaks of the invention as "a car with eight wheels, arranged and connected in the manner and acting upon the principles stated in his specification."

That the jury may not be at a loss, either as to the *manner* or *the principles* referred to, we offer the second and third prayers; having regard too, to the act of 1793, which requires the Patentee to explain the principles of his invention.

And, that the antagonism of the Plaintiff and the Defendant, as respects the construction of the specification, may admit of no question, the fourth prayer is offered, although the necessity for it is really obviated by the prayers that precede it.

ARGUMENT.

The language of the second and third prayers is carefully copied from the specification: the fourth is taken from the latter portion of Judge Taney's first instruction in the Maryland case, inserting, in place of the defences relied on at that time, the defences set up here.*

The Plaintiff's *Second* Prayer.

"That the *manner* of the arrangement and connection above referred to is to place upon two bearing carriages, as described in the specification, the body of the passenger or other car therein mentioned—the bolsters of the bearing carriages and car body respectively being connected together by a centre pin or bolt, allowing them to swivel upon each other, and the bolsters, being either so far within the ends of the body, so as to bring all the wheels under it, or at or near the ends of the body, or so far without as to allow the latter to hang down between the bearing carriages."

The Plaintiff's *Third* Prayer.

"That the principle set forth in the specification, upon which the arrangement and connection are to effect the object aimed at, is—that by the contiguity of the fore and hind wheels of each bearing carriage, the lateral friction of the rubbing of the flanches against the rails, is *avoided*, while at the same time, the two bearing carriages, being at any desirable distance apart, consistent with the required strength of the body of the car, the advantages attendant upon placing the axles of a four-wheeled car far apart, are *obtained*."

The Plaintiff's *Fourth* Prayer.

"That the Plaintiff does not claim to be the inventor of a

* Copies of the Prayers had been handed to the Judge before the summing up commenced.

combination consisting of three elements, to wit—'the closeness of the wheels, the connection of those wheels by a long spring, and the bearing of the weight of the load exclusively upon the centre,' 'for the purpose of carrying the load smoothly, saving friction upon the road, and enabling the cars to turn the curves.' But he does claim as his invention the manner of arranging and connecting the eight wheels as specified in his patent for the object referred to in the first of these inventions, and also the connection of a rail road carriage body with them adapted either to the transportation of merchandize or of passengers."

Addressing myself to you, then, gentlemen of the jury, I shall assume that his Honor will instruct you according to the tenor of the propositions submitted to him, and the argument of which I cheerfully forbear, at the suggestion of the Court.

But it is not the Court alone that has to deal with the specification. The jury has its functions in regard to it.

The specification, to be a good one, must contain such a description as will enable a person, skilled in the art of car building, to make the car patented as a whole—a matter of which the jury are to judge from the testimony.

And the jury must be satisfied, that the specification contains a correct explanation of the principles of the invention, and also of the modes of its operation.

The Defendants insist, that the specification is defective in both these particulars.

As regards the description addressed to the car builder, they say,

First.—That no length of body is given.

Second.—Nor any precise distance between the truck wheels.

Third.—Nor any precise distance between the trucks, nor between the trucks and the ends of the body.

Fourth.—Nor any mode of draft.

Then, as regards the explanation of the principles of the specification, the Defendants say, that the explanation attempted there is false, and calculated to mislead, instead of instructing the public.

First. Because friction on curves is, in point of fact, independent of the proximity of the truck wheels—while the Patentee says the contrary.

Second. Because the free swivelling trucks that are recommended are injurious.

Third. Because the axles, instead of being as near together as circumstances will permit, according to the specification, should be as far apart as the distance between the rails.

Fourth. Because the long spring of the Patentee's proposed construction is vicious and unsafe.

Fifth. Because it is false, that length of body is necessary to ease of motion.

Sixth. Because it is better to draw by the trucks, than to permit the free swivelling that the specification, in its whole scope, recommends.

It would be easy, gentlemen, to shew you that many of these objections are either captious, or have nothing to do with the case. But it is easier to answer them, on the supposition that all are relevant.

Before you undertake to construe the specification, you must lay down some general rule to go by.

There are two modes. One is the Defendants, which

consists in picking out words and phrases, without any regard to what has gone before, or comes after, or the immediate connection of the particular sentence. It is a method of construction that would justify that edition of the Bible, where the word "not" was omitted in the seventh commandment.

The other is to take the specification as a whole, read it through, look at its words in their common acceptation, and then, before you form your judgment, recall the impression it has made upon your minds. This is the course that you pursue on all other occasions where you read that you may be informed; and I take it for granted, that, as it is a course suggested by common sense, you will not depart from it under your present responsibilities.

Taking up, now, the objections of the defence, in their order, I proceed:—

The first is, that no length of body is given.

But is not the main idea of the specification, a car to be supported on eight wheels: and are not the considerations involved in this declared, in terms, to be comfort, safety and economy: and would either comfort or economy be promoted by putting eight wheels under a car of the usual length of a four-wheeled car? Comfort, we say; so far as it depends on ease of motion, increases with the length of the car; and as regards economy, unless the number of passengers can be multiplied thereby, the addition of eight wheels is a most unnecessary expense. Indeed, doubling the length accompanies the idea of doubling the number of wheels, as the shadow accompanies the substance. The testimony of Mr. Renwick, clear and conclusive throughout, was especially so on this point. It is corroborated, too, by the experience of the country; for, wherever eight wheels

110   ARGUMENT.

are used, there the car body is invariably double the length, or more, of the ordinary four-wheeled car.

But we are not left to inference on this point. The Patentee tells us in words,

"The body of the passenger, or other car, I make of *double the ordinary length* of those which run on four wheels, and *capable of carrying double their load.*" Folio 23.

Again, having reference to length, he says,

"Because the closeness of the fore and hind wheels of each bearing carriage, taken in connection with the use of two bearing carriages, *coupled remotely from each other, as can conveniently be done, for the support of one body.*" Folio 26.

Again, at folio 27:

"For by the contiguity of the fore and hind wheels of each bearing carriage, *while the two bearing carriages may be at any desirable distance apart.*"

Again, folio 28:

"And as these two bearing carriages may be placed at any distance from each other, consistent with the required strength of the body of the car."

It seems, then, there can be no doubt that length, with its consequential advantages, was a leading idea in the mind of the Patentee.

The objection, however, admitting this for the sake of the argument, insists, that this length should be defined, by which we understand, expressed in feet and inches.

In place of feet and inches, however, a better standard, addressed to those for whom the specification is more especially intended, is given, when they are told to make the car of double the ordinary length, where they propose to put it upon double the ordinary number of wheels;—that

ARGUMENT. 111

is to say, to make an eight-wheel passenger car, double the ordinary length of a four-wheeled passenger car, and an eight-wheeled burden car, double the ordinary length of a four-wheeled burden car.

I take it for granted, that the gentleman from Massachusetts is too good a lawyer to pretend, that, if the Patentee had given a length, in feet and inches,—thirty feet for instance,—a builder, who had made a car thirty-one feet in length, would find, in the additional foot, a shield against the consequences of infringement. Certainly not. In such a case the Court would leave it to the jury to say, whether the variation from the terms of the specification, was colorable or substantial,—whether the Defendant, in what he had done, "had taken," in the words of an eminent English Judge, "a leaf out of the Plaintiff's book." So, here, the instruction of the Court to you, gentlemen of the jury, will be assumed to be, that the reference to a standard that was well known, was a sufficient indication of the length of the car; and that if the Defendants, in this respect, have availed themselves of the Plaintiff's instructions, as contained in the specification, they are responsible to him.

Branching, afterwards, from the main idea of their objection, the Defendants insist, that if there is any description in regard to length, it has been exceeded,—their cars being more than double the ordinary length; such being the case indeed with the eight-wheeled cars all over the country.

The development of the Plaintiff's idea, however, were there, otherwise, a foundation for this branch of the objection, would not lessen the responsibility of those who had made use of it as the ground-work of their operations.—

The invention was complete in this regard, when doubling the length for the purposes indicated, was suggested.— Mere increase of length, afterwards, involved no new invention—suggested no new principle.

But, the specification settles this question. The Patentee tells you, that "the bearing carriages may be placed at any distance from each other, *consistent with the required strength of the body of the car.*" Here, then, is the clearest indication, that the car body may be as long as the strength of the materials employed will admit,—and this is a conclusive answer to the objection.

We, therefore, contend, that a description of the length, in feet and inches, is unnecessary.

First. Because there is a sufficient reference in the specification to a well known standard.

Second. Because, although this standard varies according to circumstances, and the taste and fashion of builders, it still remains a certain one, in view of the exigencies of the case.

Third. Because the specification looks to any increase of length, consistent with the strength of the materials.

But the following passage in the specification is relied on to shew, that, notwithstanding all that is here said, *length of body* was an unimportant consideration in the Plaintiff's mind.

"When the bolsters of the bearing carriages are placed under the extreme ends of the body, the relief from shocks and concussions, and from lateral vibrations, is greater than it is when the bolsters are placed between the middle and the ends of the body; and this relief is not materially varied by increasing or diminishing the length of the body, while the extreme ends of it continue to rest on the bolsters of the bearing cars, the load being supposed to be equally distributed over the entire length of the body."

This, however, is the statement of a mechanical truth having express reference to the car that he describes,—a car of double the ordinary length, capable of carrying double the ordinary load, and capable of being increased to any length consistent with the required strength of the materials,—a statement not controlling, by any means, the scope and spirit of the specification.

The object of the Patentee is to justify, so to speak, the location of his trucks under the extremities of the body, and to compare the advantages of this position, with the position between the middle and the ends of the body. A diagram, exaggerated purposely for illustration sake, will explain this, at once, while, at the same time, it illustrates a fallacy of the argument of the learned counsel in regard to the inferences to be drawn from the fact, that, whatever the jolt at the end of a car, the effect to raise the *centre* of the car is the same, irrespective of the length of the body.*
(The diagram referred to, is in the note below.)

---

* In the diagram, the line, from A to B, represents the length of a car body. G G', are the centres of the trucks, mid-way between the middle and the ends. Let an obstacle, now, at G', throw up the centre to H. The amount of the disturbance of the whole mass will be represented by the area of the triangles A F G, and G I B. But let the truck centres be at the extremities of the body A and B. Then the same disturbing cause at B, throwing up the end of the body to O, the whole disturbance will be represented by the triangle A O B, which mere inspection shows to be less than the sum of the other two. Now, suppose the same body lengthened at each end, to D and L; and the same disturbance to take place, where the truck is between the middle and the ends, at G', and the amount of additional disturbance is represented by the areas I B L K, and D A F

114 ARGUMENT.

The same diagram demonstrates, also, the fallacy of the idea, that because the disturbance of the central point always remains the same, whether the car be a long or a short one, therefore, the lengthening of the body cannot affect the ease of motion, while the trucks remain at or near the ends.

The second objection to the sufficiency of the specification is,—

That the precise distance between the truck wheels is not given, because not expressed in feet and inches.

It is also objected here, that the directions are peremptory,—because the truck wheels are required to be *very near* together.

The parts of the specification, where the position of the truck wheels is mentioned, are, folio 21, where it is said, "the two wheels on either side of these carriages are to be placed *very near* to each other. The spaces between these flanches *need be* no greater than is necessary to prevent their contact with each other:" again, in folio 26, where the common bearing carriage is mentioned, as an alternative construction, "provided the fore and hind wheels

E. But, suppose the trucks in this case, to be at the extremities L and D,—and the end L be thrown up to M, then the additional disturbance is measured by the areas D A C' and P B L M, deducting the triangle C O P, which is far less than the foregoing, as is apparent at a glance.

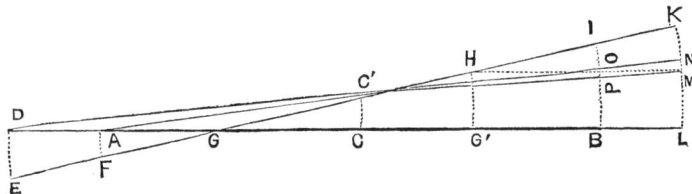

of each of them be placed *very near* together, because *the closeness of the fore and hind wheels* of each bearing carriage, taken in connection with the use of two bearing carriages, coupled remotely from each other, as can conveniently be done, for the support of one body, with a view to the objects and on the principles hereinbefore set forth, is considered by me as a most important feature of my invention: for by the *contiguity of the fore and hind wheels of each bearing carriage*, which the two bearing carriages may be at any desirable distance apart, the lateral friction from the rubbing of the flanches against the rail is most effectually avoided, whilst at the same time, all the advantages attendant upon placing the axles of a four-wheeled carriage far apart, are thus obtained," and again, at folio 28, "the two wheels on either side of one of the four-wheeled bearing carriages may, from their proximity be considered as acting *as a single wheel.*"

There are certainly no dimensions, in feet and inches, given in these extracts, which it is believed are all that the specification contains on this point. But were such dimensions necessary? This is the question.

Admitting the specification to be, in all other respects sufficient, does the omission complained of invalidate it.

This depends, in turn, upon the question, whether the public are deprived of the benefit of the invention without it. Is it of the essence of the invention, that the distance between the flanches of the wheels should be defined by exact measurements? Let us see.

It is very evident, that the Patentee has one leading thought in this connection,—a mathematical, and controlling truth. It is, that upon the curvatures of short radius to which he refers, the closer the wheels are together, and the nearer their axles conform to the radii of curvations, the less is the friction between the flanches of the wheels and the rails: and it is equally clear, that, inasmuch as it was this friction in a four-wheeled car, which suggested the invention to him, he desires to have as little of it as possible in the new construction;—in other words, he desires to have the wheels so close together, that they may be considered *as acting as a single wheel:* and when he tells the car builder this, as he has done in the specification, has he not given him the information necessary to enable him to construct the car in the best manner, for the particular road on which it is to run?

He says to him in effect, "the distance between the axles of four-wheeled cars, heretofore, has varied, from three and a half to five feet, *according 'to the nature of the road'* on which they have been running. By using two bearing carriages under an eight-wheeled car, you will be able to place the wheels much nearer than this, and so diminish the friction between the flanches of the wheels and rails. This proximity will make them act as a single wheel. They '*need be*' no farther apart than to prevent their flanches from coming in contact. To meet the exigency that is before me, (the Patentee,) consequent upon a road with curves of but a few hundred feet radius—(for the Patentee's reference to roads with such curves runs through his specification, and is never to be lost sight of,) to meet this exigency, I place the wheels very near together. This, with me, makes them act as a single wheel."

In truth, this was the only instruction that could be given. The Patentee explained the principle and described a mode by which he had carried it out on roads with curvatures of but a few hundred feet radius. His specification then, is not merely the enunciation of a principle, but a principle with an accompanying and practical illustration.

Suppose that an exact measurement had been given—thirty-two inches between the *centres* of the axles, for instance. This would have done where thirty inch wheels were used; but it would not have answered for thirty-three inch wheels; and had the road been one of extremely "sharp" curves, such as the Quincy Road, using eighteen inch wheels, it would have been more than was consistent with the principle of the invention.

Again, the exact measurement, which would have made the two wheels act as one, on a curve of four hundred feet radius, would be shorter than might be required to produce the same effect on a curve of fifteen hundred feet radius, did that happen to be the smallest radius of curvature on the particular road.

Again, while on a road of large radii of curvature, wheels close together, according to the exact measurement, might do well, yet circumstances, such for instance as the introduction of the swinging bolster, might require the distance between the centres of the axles to be increased, when, although the two wheels, owing to the large curvatures, might still act as one wheel, and all the benefit of the invention accrue to the owner of the car, yet the patent might be evaded, because the exact dimensions were not adopted,—which cannot be law.

So that we are brought back to the point from which we started, which was the enquiry whether this invention belonged to that class, whose essence was to be found in a peculiar form—illustrated by the case in 2nd Brockenbrough, 298, of Davis *vs.* Palmer—or exact dimensions. We trust that we have shewn the contrary; and that the clear explanation of the principle which the specification contains, along with the description of a car illustrating it in practice on a given road, will be looked upon as gratifying all the requisitions of the law under which the Plaintiff claims.

But, as already said, while on the one hand, the defence is, that the specification is not sufficiently exact, on the other hand, it is said, that it is so exact as to permit no departure from its directions; and that because the wheels of the Defendants' cars are not *"very near"* together, but have a swinging bolster between them, there can be no recovery on the plea of the general issue. This is Mr. Waterman's view of the specification. But Mr. Copeland, when he referred, in his cross-examination, on this very point, to the words *"need be,"* in the sentence, "the spaces between their flanches *need be* no greater than is necessary to prevent their contact with each other," answered and removed this objection altogether. These two words qualify all that is said upon the subject of the proximity of the wheels, and shew, conclusively, that the direction is not imperative; but that the distance is referred to the discretion of the car builder, to be settled by him according to the exigency of circumstances, always keeping in view the result aimed at,—to wit, the saving of the friction in the truck of the eight-wheeled car, that is inevitable in a car on four wheels, "the distance" between whose wheels, is "governed by the nature of the road on which it runs, and other considerations."

The experience of the rail road world, in this country, corroborates these views. There is not an eight-wheeled passenger car to be found anywhere, whose truck wheels would not, at a glance, be described as *"very near"* together by any one who had ever seen a passenger car on four wheels. "Very near" is comparative. As already said, in another connection, the four and eight wheel cars, that pass the curves of Grand and Centre Streets, in this city, illustrate its meaning.

The jury have the specification before them, and they see daily the Defendants' cars in actual use. The question will be whether, constructed as they are, they violate the Plaintiff's patent.

Then comes the third objection to the description of the specification,—that it does not define exactly the distance between the trucks and the ends of the body of the car.

Gentlemen, I shall not dwell on this point.—The specification gives three positions for the trucks—at the end of the body—near the end of the body—outside the end of the body, with the car suspended between the trucks.

There seems to have been a very clear intelligence at work in prescribing these alternatives. The two first meet, most aptly, all subsequent developments in regard to the lengthening of the body. Many measurements have been made and offered in evidence. I have them before me. I see, here, that where a car is forty-two feet in length, the truck centres are five feet one inch from the end. Where a car is thirty-five feet five inches long, the truck centre is four feet from the end. It is evident, that the framing of the bodies has influenced this difference. But these cars shew the propriety of the direction given to the car builder by the words "at or near;" and it is presumed, that no one will deny, that both of them are strictly within that principle of the specification, which is the soul of the patent,—the closeness of the wheels of the trucks and the remoteness of the trucks from each other.

Gentlemen, there can be no better place than this, to notice the peculiar cross-examination to which the Plaintiff's witnesses were subjected, in regard to these matters of length of body, and closeness of wheels, and position of trucks. I do not intend to repeat any of the questions of the learned counsel from Massachusetts: but his plan was to bring the witness down, foot by foot, and inch by inch, accompanying each fresh dimension with a question as to the similarity of the hypothetical construction with the car described in the specification. Gentlemen, there was not a witness that did not readily admit that there was a point, at which such small advantage would be taken of the Patentee's suggestion, that it would be difficult to say, whether there was an infringement or not. And nothing more than this, which no reasonable man could be found to deny, resulted from a cross-examination, which, to say the least of it, was not a brief one. Gentlemen, who can doubt that there must be this difficulty in every case that appears before you. To come as close as possible without infringing is often the study of skill and intelligence when a patent is to be evaded. I might illustrate for a week by references to cases. But, gentlemen of the jury, it is this very thing which you, and nearly all juries in patent cases, are empannelled to try,—with this advantage, on our side, however, on this occasion,—that no hypotheses present themselves here to trouble you, but a plain matter of fact, whether the cars actually used by the Defendants, varying in length from thirty-five to forty-five feet, with trucks whose distance apart varies from twenty-seven to thirty-five feet, and the axles of whose wheels are from two feet ten to four feet two asunder, are in violation of a specification, whose essence is the *closeness* of the wheels of trucks, coupled *remotely* from each other, at or near the ends of the body. About this as a fact, and not an hypothesis, we trust, gentlemen of the jury, you will have no difficulty.

In connection with the argument here made, we offer the following prayers—the fifth and sixth presented by us—for the instruction of the Court:—

The fifth prayer is taken mainly from the opinion of Judge Nelson, and leaves it to the jury to say, whether the instructions of the specification are sufficient to enable a person skilled in the art to build the car. The sixth follows the language of Chief Justice Taney, in regard to the necessity of describing what was before known.*

The Plaintiff's *Fifth* Prayer.

"That the improvement does not consist in placing the two bearing carriages at any precise distance apart, or from each end of the body in the construction of the car,—this distance depending necessarily, somewhat, upon the length of the car, and the strength of the materials of which it is constructed;—provided, said bearing carriages be at or near the end of a body of the length described in the specification; and that, therefore, the patent is not invalid, because the Patentee does not specify such precise distances;—provided, the jury shall believe that a person skilled in the art of constructing rail road cars, would be enabled, by the description given, to construct an eight-wheeled car, with such an adjustment or arrangement of the wheels and axles as shall cause the body to pursue a more smooth, even, direct and safe course, both over the curved and straight parts of a rail road, upon the principles stated in the specification."

* These prayers were not argued, after the intimation from the Court already referred to. A portion of the argument that would have been urged in their support, is incorporated in the address to the jury here given.

The Plaintiff's *Sixth* prayer.

"That the two bearing carriages mentioned in this specification, and the other elements which form portions of the machine, which the Patentee claims to have invented, being well known and in common use, it was unnecessary to describe particularly the mode of their construction: and as he specifies what he claims as new, every other mechanical principle or combination which he mentions in his specification, and which form component parts of the machine of which he claims to be the inventor, must, by necessary implication, be considered as admitted to be old, or in use before;—and the patent, therefore, is not invalid, because he has not, in express words, stated them to be old, nor described the manner of their construction."

And now, gentlemen of the jury, that I may illustrate to you the sufficiency of the instructions contained in the specification addressed to car builders, I propose to become one myself for the occasion; and from this pile of wheels and axles, springs, bolsters and bodies, to put together, piece by piece, as I read sentence by sentence of the instrument, an eight-wheeled car,—first with spring trucks,—afterwards, with the alternative construction,—building first the bearing carriages, and afterwards placing the body upon them. And I invite your criticism, and that of my learned friend on the other side, that I may be corrected, if I use a word that is not found in the specification, or do a thing that is not directed to be done there.

(And, accordingly, Mr. Latrobe constructed the model of an eight-wheeled car from the materials.)

There, gentlemen of the jury, you see the car. And now, I pray you, tell me how is it to be drawn? Where, in the name of common sense, is the draft to be applied? Where would a car builder, who had done, in full size, what I have done with these toys, place the draw pin? On the body, or on the truck? Where could he place it, gentlemen, but on the body? Look for yourselves, and see.

Can I reply more thoroughly and conclusively than I here do to the fourth objection, that the specification describes no place to draw from? But the specification is *not* silent. The preferred construction, with long springs, does not permit a draft by the truck. The spirit of the specification is, that the trucks shall traverse the curves with the least friction,—and this is inconsistent with a draft by the truck, which would restrict free motion. Couple, then, these particulars with the directions for construction, and how it can be doubted, that the draft is intended to be by the body, I cannot see.

But, gentlemen, we have the drawing filed in 1838, and that is conclusive. It corresponds with the testimony, as to what, in fact, was the mode of draft in the perfected car. It meets all the requisitions of construction, and it illustrates the only mode by which the principles of the specification could be made available.

And in connection with this part of my argument, I offer to the Court the following prayer:—

The Plaintiff's *Seventh* prayer.

"That the Plaintiff does not claim any particular mode in the specification, of drawing the eight-wheeled car described therein: but the specification contains nothing that is inconsistent with the draft being by the body, and not by the bearing carriages,—and the drawings filed by the Patentee on the 19th November, 1838, shewing the draft to be by the body, are prima facie evidence of the particulars of the invention, and the patent granted therefor in 1834."

And thus, gentlemen, I conclude my argument as it relates to the Defendants' objections to the sufficiency of the specification, in view of its instructions to those skilled in the art of car building.

The act of 1793, which governs the specification in this case, declares, that "in the case of any machine, the Patentee shall fully explain the principles and the several modes in which he has contemplated the application of that principle by which it may be distinguished from other inventions."

The Defendants' deny that we have done this. Let us now examine their objections.

First. The theory of the specification is, that the proximity of the wheels of the trucks is important in facilitating the passage of curves of small radius. Our opponents deny this; or if they admit it to any extent, they deny that any practical benefit results from the proximity of the truck wheels. On the contrary, they insist that the construction that we recommend is dangerous to human life; that the truck wheels when placed close together are more liable to leave the track; that the truck wabbles more, and that a decent precaution against accidents and a proper regard for human life require the distance between the axles to be as great as the distance between the rails.

With regard to the theory involved in this matter, gentlemen, the experiments made before you with the model of the Quincy car, relieve me from the necessity of extended argument. It is very true, as remarked, while they were going on, by the gentleman, whose weapons were being turned against him, that there is a great deal of difference between the speed at which the mimic car rolled down the mimic rail, and sixty miles an hour. But how did this alter the fact that the model exhibited, or make it less a truth. The law of nature that was illustrated remains the same at all speeds to which man can drive machinery; and the question here is as regards the truth of a principle set forth in the specification.

So much for the theory. A word now about the practice among engine builders through the country. For some purpose, that I have forgotten, my learned opponent produced a drawing of an engine built by the Messrs. Norris of Philadelphia. Perhaps it was touching this very point, about the proximity of the truck wheels, for the drawing represented the axles some five feet apart. But why did not my learned friend, bring with him drawings from Boston, instead of going to Philadelphia. Look gentlemen, (said Mr. L. holding up a large lithograph,) here is the engine built by the Amoskeag Manufacturing Company—and here is another built at the Boston Locomotive Works. Could the gentlemen on the other side, with their thorough investigation of all matters bearing on this cause, have been ignorant of the facts here exhibited? Impossible. Then why not exhibit drawings like those just shewn to you, where the truck wheels are almost in contact, instead of shewing a drawing of what would seem to represent an exception to a general rule? Why leave it to us to offer in evidence the fact, that engine after engine on this very Defendants' road, has its truck wheels as close as they can be put,—and its tender wheels the same? The measurements of Mr. Slade were uncontradicted, and they put this matter beyond question.

And as to danger to life or limb! Why, if my learned

friend is right, the best counsel he can give to his neighbors in Massachusetts, is to abandon a construction which, if he can persuade them to believe the argument he has made here, will, in the event of accident resulting in death from the running off of an engine, subject them to a prosecution for murder in any Court of criminal jurisdiction—for the greater number of their engines are doubtless furnished with trucks after the fashion of the drawings I have shewn you.

Gentlemen of the jury, there can be no better comment upon the frivolousness of the argument than the practice of the country: no better commendation of the Patentee, than the almost universal adoption of the principle enunciated by him, by the best builders in the country, in the construction of the truck of the engine, the most important and responsible of the trucks that are in a train.

The *second* objection under this head is, that the free swivelling of the trucks, permitted by the Patentee's construction, is a construction false in principle, and we are told that side bearings are indispensable to control it.

Then why so many engine trucks, so many leading tender trucks, without side bearings? Why the practice, shown by Mr. Slade's measurements, on the road of these Defendants' in this regard?

Side bearings are necessary to the steadiness of the car, to prevent uncomfortable rocking. They are not wanted in the trucks of locomotives, because the engine is steadied on the driving wheels; nor on the leading truck of the tender, because there are side bearings on the hind truck: facts which shew to demonstration the unsoundness of the argument that they are essential to safety. There is not a particle of proof of an accident owing to the free swivelling

ARGUMENT. 127

of engine trucks having no side bearings, and it is to the engine the accident would occur, could such want be a cause of it.

The specification says nothing of side bearings, in the sense referred to by the defence, as means of controlling the free motion of the trucks. But the reference to the bolsters of a common road wagon, suggests necessarily such bearing as steadiness requires. The fifth wheel of every carriage is a side bearing. The king bolt itself, if reasonably tight, answers the purpose of one. The drawing of the Columbus proved by Cromwell shews a side bearing in the shape of a fifth wheel. The drawing attached to the specification shews it. When the patent was issued, the speed of engines being less than it now is, a side bearing less extended than is now used, was found sufficient. The extension of it to meet the new state of things was a matter of course.

The Comet, the Washington cars, the ten Cumberland cars spoken of by Murray, the freight cars, all ran well without such as is now commonly used.

Here again, then, there is nothing in theory or practice to support this particular objection.

We now come to the "theory of the square," as distinguished from the proximity of the trucks recommended in the specification.

This is an ingenious fancy, having neither theory nor practice to recommend it. In upwards of forty measurements on rail roads diverging from this city, on four feet eight inches, five feet, and six feet guages, not a single instance has been found where it has been observed. The practice of the country is against it, and even the Defendants' counsel abandons it, when he gives up its inflexibility, and begins to talk of a few inches more or less. Of the trucks for tenders on the Defendants' road, no less than thirteen, measured at random by Mr. Slade, had axles not exceeding two feet eleven inches apart; and of the engines, seventeen of them had trucks with axles not exceeding three feet six inches apart; and of passenger cars twenty-six out of thirty had trucks, with swinging bolsters, where the truck axles did not exceed four feet apart. So much then for the theory of the square.

This brings us to the objection to the long spring.—A great deal has been urged on this point. It is one on which the Defendants' paper experts have loved to expatiate. We will have to notice, in another place, what they swear in regard to it. At present, it suffices to say, gentlemen, that the trucks which have been brought to New York, and which have been proved by the witness, Reanie, to have been in use for years, contradict all the fine spun theories that you have heard uttered on the stand, and read from the depositions, and shew, that for simplicity of construction and durability, they fully justify the preference given to them in the specification.

Again, it is said as a distinct objection, that the Plaintiff's principle of making the four-wheeled car body double the length and upwards, when put on eight wheels, is unsound. The sufficient general answer is the universal practice of the country. The sufficient special answer is the fact, that these Defendants' cars unquestionably infringe the Plaintiff's patent in this respect. The reason for this practice is to be found in the demonstrations of the model to which I have already called your attention.

ARGUMENT. 129

With regard to the last point of objection made by the defence, the superiority of the draft by the truck, instead of the draft by the body, it will be time enough to dwell upon it, gentlemen, when the draft by the body, conforming as it does to the principle of the Plaintiff's specification, ceases to be, what it now is, universal,—the few exceptions shewn to exist confirming rather than weakening the general rule upon the subject. Had the Defendants so drawn their cars, the introduction of this objection might have been more appropriate.

I have thus shewn, that the Defendants' objections to the specification, both as regards the vagueness of its descriptions, and the falsity of its theories, are unfounded: and in doing so, I have shewn that the Patentee has sufficiently protected himself in those rights which his invention and his patent conferred upon him.

The rights of the Plaintiff as inventor, and the sufficiency of his specification, being established, this would be the proper place, gentlemen, at which to address the Court upon the question of abandonment. But his Honor has intimated his wishes in this regard, and I shall therefore, rely on his instructing you in the language of

The Plaintiff's *Eighth* prayer:—

"That if the jury believe that the Plaintiff was the true inventor of the car Columbus, and that the same was put on the Baltimore and Ohio Rail Road, in the summer of 1831, and that it was used on the said road, from time to time, and without objection on the part of the Plaintiff up, and subsequent, to the date of his patent, yet such as does not amount to an abandonment of the invention by the

Plaintiff, if the jury shall believe that the intermediate time between putting the Columbus into use, and the taking out of the patent, was devoted by the Plaintiff in good faith to the perfecting of his invention, according to his opportunities for so doing; or provided the jury shall believe, that the car Columbus was not substantially the same in the manner of arranging and connecting the eight wheels, and the principle of their action, described in the Plaintiff's specification."

This prayer puts the question of abandonment on two grounds.—First, that there could have been no abandonment, no matter what time elapsed, provided the Plaintiff was engaged, in the interval, in good faith and according to his opportunities, in prosecuting the experiments that finally resulted in the patented machine.—And again, that unless the jury shall believe, that not only the Winchester, the Dromedary, the Comet, and the Washington cars, were the same in principle and mode of operation with the car described in the specification, but that the Columbus also, was identical therewith, there was no abandonment. This was the opinion of Chief Justice Taney in the Maryland case.

Next in the order of my argument follows the question of infringement and the amount of damages.

But, before approaching this, I desire, gentlemen of the jury, to say a word or two about the written testimony with which this cause has been overloaded. Twenty experts, so to call them, from different quarters of the compass, have been examined under commissions; and although not in this cause, yet by agreement of counsel, and under the ruling of the Court, you have heard what they have had to say in regard to the many matters involved in this investigation. They are the parties that the Plaintiff's counsel struggled, unsuccessfully, to have brought upon *the stand*. Dealing with them in the aggregate, it may be said that they dilate with more or less diffuseness upon several topics.

They tell us, in the first place, what *cannot* be done; when they attack the Plaintiff's construction of his car.

Then they tell us what *ought* to be done; when they indulge in theories of their own.

Again, we are informed of what *might* be done; under which head we generally have an eulogy of Chapman.

And closing their dissertations with an account of what *has been* done, they attribute it all to this "noble Englishman," as he is called by the gentleman from Massachusetts.

I cannot consume the brief space that remains to me, for the Court has announced that the argument must close to-day, with the unprofitable labor of examining *seriatim*, the testimony of these gentlemen. Dealing with them in the general, I may remark, however,

In the first place, that what they say *cannot be* done,— I instance spring trucks,—has been done:

To what they say *ought to* be done,—I instance the square of the track,—has rarely ever been done, even by the Defendants:

That what they say *might* have been done, on Chapman's teaching, has never yet been done where Chapman taught:

And that what they say *has* been done in America because of Chapman's work, was not done here in fact until several years after Winans had demonstrated the value of it, and after more than a quarter of a century had elapsed from Chapman's publication.

But they deserve, perhaps, more particular attention. Let me, therefore, take one of them, Mr. Samuel Cooper. I select him for several reasons.

First, because his testimony is a clever book by itself, of forty pages of large octavo.

Again, because his testimony is certainly the most confidently given.

Again, because he is the townsman of the gentleman from Massachusetts.

And again, because enough has transpired in this cause to shew, that either Mr. Whiting learned what he knows from Mr. Cooper, or that he suggested to Mr. Cooper the current of the thought that took the direction pursued in the testimony.

Mr. Cooper is not only very voluminous both in the number of points touched upon, but he is very diffuse in his details. So much so, that, finding the examination-in-chief did not afford him opportunities to tell all he knew, he availed himself of the cross-examination to let out the balance: a fact, gentlemen, that accounts, perhaps, for the great readiness of our friends on the other side to admit the cross-examination of their witnesses generally, after the Court had ruled in the examination-in-chief.

I will refer to Mr. Cooper, however, but on a single point. The long side springs connecting the truck wheels, and their appurtenances. My object is to test Mr. Cooper's reliability, as a witness. I cannot do this better in the case of an expert, than to test his opinions by facts. If I can prove a fact beyond all controversy—if I can make it visible and tangible to the jury,—and shew to you that, in the opinion of the individual, it is an impossibility—why, gentlemen, while he may be a very honest citizen and good man, he must expect to be looked upon as a very sorry expert. I propose to deal thus with Mr. Samuel Cooper: and to do so, go to the long side springs.

ARGUMENT. 133

The side springs are very clearly described in the specification. It is in proof that the Comet was built with them, and was a successful car. It is in proof that ten passenger cars, used for many years between Baltimore and Cumberland, were built with them. It is proved that an hundred burthen cars, and more, were built with them on the Baltimore Road, and ran unaltered for years. It is proved that on that road, after trying other trucks, the Master of Machinery is going back to the spring truck for his locomotives, as the best sort of truck. It is proved that twenty-six hundred cars, passenger and burden, have been built with them in Russia, where they are in constant use. It has been shewn that engine on engine, in the neighborhood of Boston, even, have spring trucks; and above all, spring trucks, in exact accordance with the specification, with brakes and without brakes, have been taken from under cars and engines, and have been brought by the Plaintiff to New York and placed in the Park, where they have been identified by proof; where the jury have seen them for themselves, have tried the brakes, counted the leaves of the springs, and marked the effect upon them of wear and tear. So much for the fact.

Now for the opinion of Mr. Samuel Cooper.

At one page (1052) of his testimony, he swears that the construction with spring trucks, is unsafe and *"impracticable."* Again, that it is vicious and *unsafe.* Again; that "it *is not possible* for springs to be springs and trucks both." Again, that "it is *impossible* to apply a brake to springs." Again, that "these are all *fatal* objections to springs;"—and again, that, in his opinion, spring trucks are "entirely unsafe and *impracticable."*

There is but one way of extricating Mr. Cooper from his

18

antagonism with facts, which is to suppose him to be very badly informed, or very ignorant of the force of the language that he is pleased to use. Did dogmatism need illustration, Mr. Cooper's deposition would furnish it.

Now, what is such testimony worth? What the value of opinions thus pronounced? Mr. Cooper says that he has never been on the stand as a witness. In some degree, this accounts for his uncommon faculty of emphasis. A day passed by him between my brother Keller and my learned opponent, under oral examination, would perhaps somewhat qualify this peculiar faculty. So much for Mr. Cooper.

But there is a word or two to be said about the getting up of all this testimony, irrespective of its quality.

There was a good deal of this sort of work to be done: and labor-saving contrivances are it seems, above all others, appreciated by parties familiar with patent cases.

I have not had time to go over the printed testimony in detail; but my brother Sickles, whose untiring industry is an example to us all, has done so faithfully; and from his very full brief, I have ascertained that a portion of the testimony is but a succession of echoes.

I select a few instances to illustrate this from Mr. Sickles' brief.

Warden, of Troy, a car builder, copies Farley, of Boston, an engineer, in his answer to the sixth interrogatory for twenty-two lines, word for word.

Young, an engineer, of New York, copies Farley in his answer to the thirteenth interrogatory for forty-two lines, word for word.

Pettit, of Philadelphia, and Smith and Shryack, of Baltimore, are identical in their answers to the sixteenth interrogatory for seven lines, word for word.

ARGUMENT. 135

Farley is copied by Wilkinson, of Syracuse, formerly President of the New York Central Rail Road, for twenty-six lines, word for word.

Farley, Worden and Wilkinson are identical in the answer to the twenty-seventh interrogatory, for forty-two lines, word for word.

My learned opponent, who was aware, before he made his argument, of this discovery, and desired to anticipate the effect of its disclosure, made some attempts to do so, which I confess I was not able entirely to appreciate. He seemed to look upon what had been done as quite justifiable. I hardly thought, however, that his explanations were as happy as usual.

But, gentlemen of the jury, what is the language of the commission from the Court in Boston, under which this testimony was taken.

"N. B. You shall not, except by the consent of the parties in writing, permit either party to attend at the taking of the depositions, either himself, or by any attorney or agent, nor to communicate by interrogatories or suggestions with the deponents, whilst giving their depositions or answers to the interrogatories annexed to this commission. And you shall take such depositions in a place separate and apart from all other persons, and permit no person to be present during such examination except the deponents and yourself, and such disinterested person (if any) as you may think fit to appoint as a clerk to assist you in reducing the depositions to writing: and you shall put the several interrogatories and cross-interrogatories to the deponents in their order, and take the answer of the deponents to each fully and fairly."

The scope and spirit of these instructions are, that the

witness shall hear the question from the commissioner, and give his answer in his own words, at that time, without aid or prompting from any quarter. Had this been done, it would have been nothing short of a miracle had the coincidence of language referred to taken place. But, no, gentlemen of the jury, the whole thing is perfectly intelligible. There have been one or more agents at work in the preparation of this case. He or they have not been present before the commissioner; but the inference is irresistible that in many instances they have furnished the witnesses copies of the interrogatories,—have shown them what other witnesses have sworn,—have written out their testimony for them, or gotten the witnesses to do so themselves, on their prompting; and finally, when fully prepared, have sent them before the commissioner—some of them, like Mr. Cooper, with a treatise and references to authorities, all cut and dried—to swear loosely and inconsiderately, or wisely and well, as the case might be.

Some of these witnesses seem to have been fastidious,—unwilling to *appear* to parrot a lesson; and they have inverted answers and transposed sentences, that the copying might be concealed; at all events, they have done that which justifies this being said of them.

I illustrate this, gentlemen, by referring to the answers of Messrs. Wilkinson and Farley, to the twenty-seventh interrogatory.

A singular piece of patch-work, you will find this to be. (Mr. Latrobe here handed to the Court, and to one of the jury, copies of the printed testimony, that his quotations might be verified.)

The first sentence of Wilkinson's answer is the seventh of Farley's—the second is Farley's sixth—the third his fourth—the fourth of Wilkinson is the fifth of Farley—the sixth is Farley's third—the seventh is Farley's first. The eighth corresponds with Farley's ninth, and the ninth of Wilkinson is identical with the eighth of Farley. With the exception of about half a dozen words, if so many, the transposition here noticed has been effected without the loss of a syllable even. Not an idea is modified, either, by the change in the position of the sentences.

Now how can this be explained? I leave it to others better versed than I am fortunate enough to be in the getting up of the testimony of experts. To me it is wholly unintelligible. If a copy was to be made, why was it not done frankly and avowedly, and put upon the ground of want of time, or any other bold, outspoken reason?

Gentlemen of the jury, what think you of all this. Is it in accordance with your notions of right. Is it fair. Is it honest?

But, gentlemen of the jury, this is not all. Look at this model B. (here the counsel held up the Defendants' model of the Plaintiff's car, referred to in the depositions of the Defendants' witnesses.) This is the Marching Lie that has been travelling over the country to aid in the production of this mass of testimony. See these springs, curved like a new moon, almost. Are these fair representations of the springs of the Defendants' truck? Under whose direction was this model made? Was it made for the purposes of truth, or of deception? If the party who ordered it had looked at the first locomotive that passed him, he would have seen the *flat horizontal springs* of its truck. Had he taken the drawing of the Comet, sworn to by the witnesses, he would have seen springs of the same shape.

What warrant, what excuse, was there, for this most wilful exaggeration? Gentlemen, I enquired for this model, while my learned opponent was speaking. He observed my doing so. Soon afterwards, he volunteered an explanation about the spring, saying, that, without curving it, as you see, there was no room for the lower bolster between the flanches. But look for yourselves, gentlemen. My learned friend is mistaken. There is ample room—ample room—as there always is, for Truth, had not the party ordering this model designed an exaggeration to prejudice the Plaintiff's case.

Why dwell I upon this? Because of the stress laid by the Defendants, as you have heard, upon the peculiar truck, of which this spring forms part. Because it is insisted, that to this spring truck alone has the Plaintiff any claim.—Because this spring is one of the three elements, which, it is said, when combined, make up the invention. Because, in the shape in which it is used, and which this model should have given to it, the elasticity of the spring causes no deviation from parallelism in the axles that is appreciable; whereas, in this new moon form, the spring truck would indeed be an absurdity; and because, finally, I desired to shew you, that this palpable falsehood was palmed on witness after witness, not inconsiderately and accidentally, but because of the influence it was supposed it might exercise upon the case.

Gentlemen of the jury—the testimony in favor of the Defendants, has indeed been "gotten up." And were not the counsel for the Plaintiff therefore fully justified in every effort that they made to have such testimony excluded?

Gentlemen, in regard to the witnesses for the defence, with few and unimportant exceptions, you had them all upon the stand. Their testimony must stand or fall by the impression that it made upon you. You saw and heard for yourselves.

Let me now say a few words in regard to the question of infringement, and the amount of damages. Here is the Defendants' own model of the car they use. The cars themselves pass you daily in the streets of your city. After the Court shall have instructed you upon the construction of the specification, you will have no difficulty, I am sure, on this point, about your verdict.

Then comes the damages. What are they to be? They are laid in the declaration at ten thousand dollars. The smallest patent fee you could allow would far exceed this sum, when multiplied by the number of eight-wheeled cars in use, prior to the commencement of this action, and that again by the number of years—admitting even, which I am by no means prepared to do, that the statute of limitations can be made available under the plea of the general issue. About the amount of your verdict then, should you be able to agree upon one for the Plaintiff, there can be no doubt. The whole of it will be insufficient to cover the expenses of this single suit. That my client is entitled to a verdict at your hands, I do, from my inmost heart, believe. That the country is indebted to him for this great invention has, I respectfully submit, been most conclusively established. That the various improvements in connection with the eight-wheeled car, which the last few years have developed, are but illustrations of its capabilities, we have had occasion, again and again, to prove to you in the course of the present trial; and in submitting the case to your decision, we feel that it is in the hands of those, upon whose ears all

140   ARGUMENT.

that has been suggested about injury to the great city of New York should there be a verdict for the Plaintiff,—all the attempts that have been made to cause Self to war with Truth, within your breasts during the last two months, have fallen as idle wind.

Gentlemen, I do not stop to thank you. I have only to say that your bearing throughout this protracted controversy has satisfied me, that I was indeed before a jury of my country, worthy of the name: and whatever may be your verdict, I shall think so still.

APPENDIX.

SCHEDULE "A."

The Schedule referred to in these Letters Patent, and making part of the same, containing a description, in the words of the said Ross Winans *himself, of his improvement in the construction of Cars or Carriages, intended to run upon Rail Roads.*

To all whom it may concern:—Be it known, that I, Ross Winans, Civil Engineer of the City of Baltimore, in the State of Maryland, have invented a new and useful improvement in the construction of cars or carriages, intended to travel upon rail roads; which improvement is particularly adapted to passenger cars, as will more fully appear by an exposition of the difficulties heretofore experienced in the running of such cars at high velocities, which exposition I think it best to give in this specification, for the purpose of exemplifying the more clearly the object of my said improvement.

Improvement in the construction of cars or carriages.

Passenger cars.

High velocities, cause of difficulties.

142   APPENDIX.

Rail roads in this country in view.

12 In the construction of all rail roads in this country, which extend to any considerable distance, it has been found necessary to admit of lateral curvatures, the radius *Curves of but a few hundred feet radius* of which is sometimes but a few hundred feet; and it becomes important, therefore, so to construct the cars, as to enable them to overcome the difficulties presented by *constitute the difficulties to be overcome,* such curvatures, and to adapt them for running with the least friction practicable, *with least friction on all parts of road.* upon all parts of the road. The friction to which I now allude is that which arises from the contact between the flanches of *Friction meant is between flanch and rail.* the wheels and the rails, which, when it occurs, causes a great loss of power and a rapid destruction of, or injury to, both the wheel and the rail, and is otherwise injurious.

Modern high velocities

13 The high velocities attained by the improvements made in locomotive engines, and which are not only sanctioned, but *make points formerly unimportant matter for special attention.* demanded by public opinion, render it necessary that certain points of construction and arrangement, both in the roads and wheels, which were not viewed as important at former rates of travelling, should *Momentum of load, intensity of shocks, and concussions, not to be neglected, as they render* now receive special attention. The greater momentum of the load and the intensity of the shocks and concussions, which are unavoidable, even under the best constructions, are among those circumstances which must not be neglected, as the liability to

APPENDIX. 143

accident is thereby not only greatly increased, but the consequences to be apprehended much more serious.

accident more probable—consequences more serious.

The passenger and other cars in general use upon rail roads have four wheels,—the axles of which are placed from three and a half to five feet apart; this distance being governed by the nature of the road upon which they run, and other considerations.

Common four-wheel car axles, 3½ to five feet apart, according to nature of road.

When the cars are so constructed that the axles retain their parallelism, and are at a considerable distance apart, there is a necessary tendency in the flanches of the wheels to come into contact with the rails, especially on the curvatures of least radius, as the axles then vary more from the direction of the radii. From this consideration, when taken alone, it would appear to be best to place the axles as near to each other as possible,—thus causing them to approach more nearly to the direction of the radii of the curves, and the planes of the wheels, to conform to the line of the rails.

Parallel axles—far apart—bring flanches and rails in contact, on sharp curves.

Therefore, axles near together,—

approaching radii of curvature.

There are, however, other circumstances which must not be overlooked in their constructions. I have already alluded to the increased force of the shocks from obstructions at high velocities; and, whatever care may be taken, there will be inequalities in the rails and wheels, which, though small, are numerous, and the perpetual operation

Other circumstances to be looked at.

Shocks at high velocities.

Perpetual operation of small inequalities in wheels and rails.

of which produces effects which cannot be disregarded. The greater the distance between the axles, while the length of the body remains the same, the less is the influence of these shocks or concussions; and this has led, in many instances, to the placing them in passenger cars, at or near their extreme ends. Now, however, a compromise is most commonly made between the evils resulting from a considerable separation and a near approach, as, by the modes of construction now in use, one of the advantages must be sacrificed to the other.

Greater distance apart of axles, the less the shocks, &c.

Therefore, axles placed at or near the ends.

Compromise the result.

17 But it is not to the lateral curvatures and inequalities of the road alone, that the foregoing remarks apply. The incessant vibration felt in travelling over a rail road is mainly dependant upon the vertical motion of the cars, in surmounting those numerous, though minute, obstructions which unavoidably exist. The nearer the axles are placed to each other, the greater is the effect of this motion upon the passengers, and the greater its power to derange the machinery and the road. It becomes very important, therefore, both as regards comfort, safety and economy, to devise a mode of combining the advantages derived from placing the axles at a considerable distance apart, with those of allowing them to be situated near to each other.

Incessant vertical vibrations to be considered.

The nearer the axles, the greater the effect of the vertical motion on passengers.

Important to find a mode of combining advantages of near and remote coupling, as regards comfort, safety and economy.

APPENDIX.

It has been attempted, and with some success, to correct the tendency of the flanches to come into contact with the rails on curved and other parts of the road, by making the tread of the wheel conical;—and if the travelling upon rail roads was not required to be very rapid, this would so far prove an effectual corrective, as the two rails would find diameters upon the wheels which would correspond with the difference in length,—the constant tendency to deviation being as constantly counteracted by this construction; but at high velocities, the momentum of the body in motion tends so powerfully to carry it in a right line, as to cause the wheel on the longer rail to ascend considerably above that part of the cone which corresponds therewith. The consequence of this is a continued serpentine motion, principally, but not entirely, in a lateral direction; nor is this confined to the curved parts of the road, but it exists to an equal or greater extent upon those which are straight, especially when the axles are near to each other,—the irregularities before spoken of constantly changing the direct course of the wheels, whilst there is no general curvature of the rails to counteract it. To avoid this effect, and the unpleasant motion and tendency to derangement consequent upon it, an additional motive is

18 Use of cone attempted to keep flanch from rail.

Would do at slow speed.

But not at high velocities, and why.

19 Serpentine motion with cars at high speed on curved and straight parts.

And why.

To avoid this, a motive for remote axles.

APPENDIX.

furnished for placing the axles at a considerable distance apart.

Object of invention. 20 The object of my invention is, among other things, to make such an adjustment or arrangement of the wheels and axles as shall cause the body of the car or carriage *To produce a more smooth, easy, direct and safe course.* to pursue a more smooth, even, direct and safe course, than it does as cars are ordinarily constructed, both over the curved *On curved and straight parts by* and straight parts of the road, by the before-mentioned desideratum of combining the advantages of the near and distant *Near and distant coupling.* coupling of the axles and other means to be hereinafter described.

Construction,—two bearing carriages. 21 For this purpose, I construct two bearing carriages, each with four wheels, which are to sustain the body of the passenger or other car, by placing one of them at or near each end of it, in a way to be presently described. The two wheels on either side of these carriages are to be placed very *Wheels "very near," "need be" no further than to keep flanches from contact.* near to each other: the spaces between their flanches need be no greater than is necessary to prevent their contact with each other. These wheels I connect together *Spring connection,— double usual strength.* by means of a very strong spring,—say double the usual strength employed for ordinary cars,—the ends of which springs *Ends secured to boxes.* are bolted, or otherwise secured, to the upper sides of the boxes, which rest on *Long leaves down.* 22 the journals of the axles; the longer leaves of the springs being placed downwards,

APPENDIX. 147

and surmounted by the shorter leaves.—
Having thus connected two pairs of wheels together, I unite them into a four-wheel bearing carriage, by means of their axles, and a bolster of the proper length, extending across between the two pairs of wheels, from the centre of one spring to that of the other, and securely fastened to the tops of them. This bolster must be of sufficient strength to bear a load upon its centre of four or five tons. Upon this first bolster I place another of equal strength, and connect the two together by a centre pin or bolt passing down through them, and thus allowing them to swivel or turn upon each other in the manner of the front bolster of a common road wagon. I prefer making these bolsters of wrought or cast iron;—wood, however, may be used. I prepare each of the bearing carriages in precisely the same way.

The body of the passenger or other car I make of double the ordinary length of those which run on four wheels, and capable of carrying double their load.

This body I place so as to rest its whole weight upon the two upper bolsters of the two before-mentioned bearing carriages or running gear. I sometimes place these bolsters so far within the ends of the body of the car as to bring all the wheels under it; and, in this case, lesss trength is neces-

Two pair of wheels united, make bearing carriage.

Bolster.

Strength of bolster.

Second bolster.
Centre pin.

Swivelling as in common road wagon.

Both bearing carriages prepared in same way.

23 *Body double the ordinary length and capacity.*

Rest on upper bolsters.

Sometimes all the wheels under the body.

148   APPENDIX.

Less strength of body necessary then.

sary in the car-body, than when the bolsters is situated at its extreme ends. In some cases, however, I place the bolster so far without the body of the car, at either end, as to allow the latter to hang down between the two sets of wheels, or bearing carriages, and to run, if desired, within a foot of the rails.

Sometimes body between the two sets of wheels.

24 When this is done, a strong frame-work projects out from either end of the car or carriage body, and rests upon the upper bolsters of the two bearing carriages. This last arrangement, by which the body of the car is hung so low down, manifestly affords a great security to the passengers, exempting them in a great degree from those accidents to which they are liable when the load is raised. Several bodies may be connected, or rest on a common frame, and be supported on the bearing carriage, in a manner similar to that of a single body.

Advantages of suspending body.

Several bodies may rest on a common frame.

25 When the bolsters of the bearing carriages are placed under the extreme ends of the body, the relief from shocks and concussions, and from lateral vibrations, is greater than it is when the bolsters are placed between the middle and the ends of the body; and this relief is not materially varied by increasing or diminishing the length of the body, while the extreme ends of it continue to rest on the bolsters of the bearing cars, the load being supposed to be

Bolsters at extreme ends, greater relief from shocks.

This not materially varied by increasing the length of body while bolsters at extreme ends.

APPENDIX.

equally distributed over the entire length of the body.

Although I prefer the use of a single spring to a pair of wheels as above described, instead of the ordinary spring to each wheel, and consider it as more simple, cheap, and convenient, than any other arrangement: the end which I have in view may, nevertheless, be obtained by constructing the bearing carriages in any of the modes usually practised, provided that the fore and hind wheels of each of them be placed very near together; because the closeness of the fore and hind wheels of each bearing carriage, taken in connection with the use of two bearing carriages coupled remotely from each other as can conveniently be done, for the support of one body, with a view to the objects and on the principles herein set forth, is considered by me as a most important feature of my invention; for by the contiguity of the fore and hinds wheels of each bearing carriage, while the two bearing carriages may be at any desirable distance apart, the lateral friction from the rubbing of the flanches against the rails is most effectually avoided, whilst, at the same time, all the advantages attendant upon placing the axles of a four-wheeled car far apart are thus obtained.

26 Single spring preferred.

Yet end obtained by common bearing carriage.

Provided fore and hind wheels very near together.

Closeness of wheels.

Carriages coupled remotely.

In view of objects set forth.

27 Most important feature.

Contiguity of fore and hind wheels.

While bearing carriages any desirable distance apart.

Lateral friction avoided.

Advantages of far apart axles otained

28   The bearing of the load on the centre of the bolster, which also is the centre of each bearing carriage, likewise affords great relief from the shocks occasioned by the percussions of the wheels on protuberant parts of the rails, or other objects, and from vibrations consequent to the use of coned wheels; as the lateral and vertical movements of the body of the car resulting from the above causes are much diminished. The two wheels on either side of one of the bearing carriages may, from their proximity, be considered as acting like a single wheel; and as these two bearing carriages may be placed at any distance from each other, consistent with the required strength of the body of the car, it is evident that all the advantage is obtained which results from having the two axles of a four-wheeled car at a distance from each other, whilst its inconveniences are avoided.

29   Another advantage of this car compared with those in common use, and which is viewed by me as very important, is the increased safety afforded by it to passengers; not only from the diminished liability to breakage, or derangement in the frame work, but also from the less disastrous consequences to be apprehended from the breaking of a wheel; axle, or other part of the running gear, as the

car-body depends, for its support and safety, upon a greater number of wheels, and bearing points on the road.

I do not claim, as my invention, the running of cars or carriages upon eight wheels, this having been previously done; not, however, in the manner or for the purposes herein described, but merely with a view of distributing the weight carried, more evenly upon a rail, or other road, and for objects distinct in character from those which I have had in view, as hereinbefore set forth. Nor have the wheels, when thus increased in number, been so arranged and connected with each other either by design or accident, as to accomplish this purpose. What I claim, therefore, as my invention, and for which I ask a patent, is the before-described manner of arranging and connecting the eight wheels which constitute the two bearing carriages with a rail road car, so as to accomplish the end proposed by the means set forth, or by any others which are analogous and dependent upon the same principles.

Disclaimer.

Claim.

Connection with a rail road car.

ROSS WINANS.

Witnesses—G. BROWN,
          J. H. B. LATROBE.

152   APPENDIX.

References to the annexed Drawing of Ross Winans' improvement in the construction of Cars or Carriages intended to run on Railroads, for which Letters Patent were issued, dated October 1st, 1834.

Fig. 1.—Side view of an eight-wheel car.

Fig. 2.—End view of the same.

Fig. 3.—Upper and lower bolster detached from the body and bearing-carriage.

A A—Represents the body of the car resting on the bearing-carriage B and C, as exhibited at D D, on pivots equidistant from the wheels of each bearing-carriage.

H—Represents an upper bolster of cast-iron, separate from the body of the car with its pivot X corresponding with the socket Y in the lower bolster E, also shown as separate from the bearing-carriage.

STATE OF MARYLAND, }
BALTIMORE CITY, ss.

On this nineteenth day of November, in the year eighteen hundred and thirty-eight, before me, the subscriber, a Justice of the Peace of the said State in and for the said city, personally appeared Ross Winans, and made solemn oath that he is the inventor of an improvement in the construction of cars or carriages intended to run on rail roads, for which Letters Patent of the United States were granted to him, dated the first day of October, 1834; and that the annexed drawing is, as he verily believes, a true delineation of the invention, as described in the said Letters Patent.

Sworn before

JAMES BLAIR,
Justice of Peace.

INDEX.

A.

Adams, President, Carriage of, 27.
Alexander, J. H. Testimony about the Herald, 30.
Abandonment, Prior to Invention, 38. Subsequent to, 44.
Allen Engine, 83, 84, 85, 86, 87.
Argument on Prayers prevented, 102, 103.
Act of 1793, 124.
Amoskeag Manufacturing Co. Engine, 125.
Abandonment—Prayer as to, 130.

B.

Baltimore, Western Relations of, 10, 11.
" Rail Road System in America, originated in, 11.
" Witnesses from, 48.
Brown, George, 13.
" in charge of Machinery, 14.
" his suggestion of Eight Wheels, 14.
Bennett, as to Wood Car, 24.
Baltimore Gazette, Article in, 27.
Baltimore and Ohio Rail Road Company, Agents of Plaintiff, for Experiments, 42.
Boy on Ice, 59.
Bryan, G. 76.
Body, length of, where referred to, 110.
Boston Locomotive Works, Engine, 125.
Body, draft by, 129.
B. model, Falsity of, 137.

154   INDEX.

C.

Canals, Erie and Pensylvania, 11.
Colts of Patterson, 12, 14.
Cromwell, 14, 43.
Columbus, first Drawing of, 14.
Cross-Examination of Defendants' counsel, as to Plaintiff's declarations, illustrated, 16, 17.
Cadwallader, as to Wood car, 24.
Columbus, 29.
Cromwell went to see Camden and Amboy Cars, 31.
Comet, 32.
Claridge, date of Washington Car, 34.
Carncross Car, 36.
Columbus, not the same as perfected Car, 38, 39.
Cooper, Peter, 40, 41, 57.
Canandaigua trial, 45, 46.
Conkling, Trial before, 46.
Cooperstown, Trial at, 46.
Cooper, Samuel, 48, 131.
Chapman Car, 50, 53, 4, 5, 6, 7, 8, 9.
"Comfort, Safety, and Economy," 97.
Car, as a whole, to be covered, 97.
Construction of Specification, 94, 95.
Copeland, 99.
Court's refusal to hear Argument on Prayers, 102, 103.
Car trucks before the Jury, 122.
Commission to take Testimony, form of, 135.

D.

Defence, General, 9.
Drawing, First Working Drawing of Columbus, 14.
Drawing of Columbus, given by Plaintiff to Cromwell, 17.
    "   "   " Alleged discrepancies in, 17
    "   "   " Mr. Whiting's interruption about, 17.

INDEX. 155

Drawing of Columbus, Gatch's statement in regard to, 18.
Draft in Timber car controlling the free swivelling, 24.
Dromedary, 31.
Davis' testimony as to draft, 34, 35.
Drawing first appeared in the Baltimore case, 43.
Detmold, &c. 93.
Diagram to shew the effect of the position of Truck, 71, 114.
Davis *vs.* Palmer, 117.
Drawing, prayer in regard to, 123.
Draft by body, direction, 129.
Damages, 139.

E.

Eight Wheel car, in Streets, 6, 7.
    Compared with four wheeled, 6, 7, 8.
Eight Wheels, George Brown's suggestion of, 14.
Eight Wheel car, Winans' first rough sketch of, 14.
    first working drawing of, 14.
Elgar, 14, 15.
Extension, 44.
Eaton & Gilbert, suit against, 46.
Ends of body, relation of trucks to, objection, 119.
Experts of Defendants, 131

F.

Four Wheeled car, compared with Eight Wheeled, 6, 7, 8.
Friction wheel, Winans, 12.
Fairbanks, 14.
Ferry, 14.
Forest, who is he, 19.
Foltz, 37.
Fairlamb, 50, 90, 91, 92.
Four Wheeled car, Model of, 52.
Farley's Testimony, 135, 136, 137.

G.

Gould, C. D. Agreement with, 6.
Grouped Wheels, 7.
Gim Crack, Friction Wheel, called so by Whiting, 12.
Gatch, Conduce, his business, 15.
" absence, 15.
" statement about drawing given him by Plaintiff, 18.
" his understanding as to the invention, 18, 19.
" belief that it is for a Truck, 19.
" who is he, 19.
,, as to Trussels, 27.
Glenn, 27.

H.

Herald, 30.
Hubbell, William, his argument, 49.

I.

Invention, circumstances at date of, 10.
Imlay, 37.
Intention as affecting abandonment, 39.

J.

Jervis, J. B. 30.
Jervis Engine, 88, 89, 90.
Ice, Boy on, 59, 60.

K.

Knight, 14, 15.

L.

Liverpool and Manchester Rail Road, 10, 12.
Length of Car, places where referred to, 110.
Long Spring, objection, 128.

INDEX. 157

M.

Mount Clare and Mount Clare Depot, 26.
Myers sent to Philadelphia, 37.
Massachusetts, suits in, 47.
Model, water, 60.
Model, to show advantage of long car, 74, 75.
McClurg *vs.* Kingsland, 82.
Model B. falsity of, 137.

N.

New Castle and Frenchtown Turnpike and Rail Road Co. *ats.* Winans, 40.
New Trial, motion for, 46.
"Need be" Copeland as to effect of, 118.
Nearness of truck wheels, where referred to, 114, 115.
Norris engine, 125.

O.

Original Inventor, was Plaintiff the, 10.
Originality, alleged want of, 22.

P.

Plaintiff's general heads, 9, 10.
Probabilities in favor of Winans as inventor, 21.
Pay Rolls, Trussels mentioned, 27.
Pennsylvania car, 37.
Prayers, 1st.—102.
      2nd.—106.
      3rd.—106.
      4th.—106.
      5th.—121.
      6th.—122.
      7th.—122.
      8th.—129.

158   INDEX.

Proximity of truck wheels, places where referred to, 114, 115
"   "   "   objections to, 124.
Pettit's testimony, 134.

Q.

Quincy car, 76, 78, 79, 80, 81.

R.

Rupp, who is he, 19.
Reynolds, 27.
Rupp, as to draft by body, 33.
Recapitulation, 92.
Rail Roads in America originated in Baltimore for general purposes, 11.

S.

Speculation—charge of, 5.
Street Car, 6, 7.
See-saw of Four-wheeled car, 8.
Stephenson, in competition with Winans, 13.
Superintendent of Machinery—G. Brown, 15.
Scroll shewing sequence of Cars, 33.
Suits brought by Gould, 44.
Susquehanna Rail Road Company, letter to, 44, 65.
Stevens, Samuel, 45.
Smith, G. W., criticism on Tredgold, 67.
Simplicity of invention, 93.
Specification, sufficiency of, 94, 95.
"Subterfuge," 101.
Specifications, objections to, 107.
Swivelling, free, objection, 126.
Square, theory of, objection, 127.
Spring, long, objection, 128.
"   "   use of, 132, 133.

T.

Timber Car, so called, 22.
Tressel Car, 27.
Taney, Judge, Opinion, 40.
Tredgold Car, 50, 61, 62, 63, 64, 65, 67.
" " G. W. Smith, upon, 67.
Trucks, Patent, insisted to be for, 96.
" Trucks, relation of to end of body, 119.
Theory of square, objection, 127.
Testimony, how "gotten up," 134.

V.

Victory, Car, 37.
"Very near," term of comparison, 119.

W.

Winans' personal history of, 11, 12.
    Probabilities of his being inventor, 21
Wood Car, 24.
Whistler, G. W. 30.
Winchester, 31.
Washington Cars, 33.
Waterman, 48.
Whiting, William, argument of, 49.
Wood's Treatise, 50, 67, 68.
Water Model, 61, 62.
Waterman's examination, 68, 69, 70, 71, 72, 73, 74.
Wheels of trucks, proximity of where referred to, 114, 115.
Witnesses of Defendants, 130.
Worden's testimony, 134.
Wilkinson, 135, 136, 137.
Wood first hauled on Baltimore and Ohio Rail Road, 24.

Y.

Young's Testimony, 134.